D1215388

The Epistle of Paul the Apostle to the Ephesians

by

Oliver B. Greene

THE GOSPEL HOUR, INC.
Oliver B. Greene, Founder
Box 2024, Greenville, South Carolina 29602

© Copyright 1963 by Oliver B. Greene
All rights reserved

Printed in the United States of America

First printing, 1963 — 5,000 copies
Second printing, 1964 — 5,000 copies
Third printing, 1966 — 10,000 copies
Fourth printing, 1967 — 10,000 copies
Fifth printing, 1969 — 15,000 copies
Sixth printing, 1970 — 15,000 copies
Seventh printing, 1973 — 15,000 copies
Eighth printing, 1973 — 15,000 copies
Ninth printing, 1975 — 25,000 copies
Tenth printing, 1977 — 10,000 copies
Eleventh printing, 1979 — 10,000 copies

The Epistle of Paul
the Apostle
to the Ephesians

INTRODUCTION

To me, Ephesians is the holy of holies of the Epistles. I feel in some small way as Moses must have felt when he was instructed to remove the shoes from his feet because the ground upon which he stood was holy ground. As I approach the study of the Epistle to the Ephesians, I feel that I, too, should remove the shoes from my feet because of the loftier levels of revealed spiritual truth in this jewel of the Epistles.

The Apostle Paul is the writer of the Epistle to the Ephesians. The date of this Epistle was A. D. 64 and it was written in Rome. Ephesians is the first of the Prison Letters of the Apostle Paul.

This letter, along with the Epistle to the Colossians and the Epistle to Philemon, was sent to the respective groups by Tychicus and is the most impersonal of all of Paul's letters to the churches. Bible authorities do not agree as to whether or not the words "to the Ephesians" appear in the original manuscripts. There is a division of Bible scholars concerning this matter, but whether or not this letter was directed to the Ephesians is not important in our study.

In Colossians 4:16 we read concerning the Epistle to the Laodiceans. Some Bible scholars suggest that this letter we are about to study was really directed to the Laodiceans. Other Bible authorities suggest that it was directed to both the Laodicean church *and* the church at Ephesus. Some suggest that the words "to the faithful in Christ Jesus" (Eph. 1:1b) indicate that the letter was not addressed to any particular assembly.

All Scripture is given by inspiration, and is profitable to us. The tremendous spiritual truth revealed in this Epistle is yours and mine to accept if we are members of the body of Christ through the miracle of the New Birth. The prophets of God delivered "oracles" to the people; but the apostles of Jesus Christ wrote letters to the brethren in Christ—letters that were directed to specific assemblies but carried a message to each and every individual who had become a member of the body of Christ through the new birth . . . and also a message to you and me who are nineteen hundred years this side of the penning down of these great truths. All Scripture up to the crucifixion of the Lord Jesus looks forward to the cross of Christ, and has the nation Israel primarily in view, and the blessings God promised to Abraham . . . earthly blessings in the Kingdom of Heaven on earth. But in the Epistles we read of the revealing of a great mystery: "And to make all men see what is the fellowship of the mystery, which from the beginning of the world hath been hid in God, who created all things by Jesus Christ" (Eph. 3:9). This mystery made known to Paul by revelation, was "hid in God from the very beginning." The mystery referred to here was the interval of time between the crucifixion of the Lord Jesus, His resurrection, and His coming again in glory to receive His church to meet Him in the air. In Matthew 16 Jesus prophesied concerning the church. He said to Peter, "Upon this rock I will build my church . . ." (notice it is future tense). Jesus did not say, "Upon this rock I *have built*," or "*am building*," but "WILL build" (future tense). The church had its beginning on the Day of Pentecost. Jesus announced the church to the apostles, but He did not reveal its position, its relationship, nor its privileges and its duties to God and to man.

In the Epistles Paul reveals the doctrine of the church as the Holy Ghost revealed it to him. In Paul's letters to the churches at Rome, Corinth, Galatia, Ephesus, Philippi, Colosse and Thessalonica, we find revealed to these churches (and to you and me) the unique place of the church in the purpose and plan of Almighty God. This tremendous truth was hidden "from the beginning of the world" (Eph. 3:9). It is through the inspired pen of the Apostle Paul that we know the church of the living God is not a local organization. The church of which Jesus was speaking in Matthew 16 is a living organism . . . the body of Christ, with a heavenly calling and a definite promise that the church will be caught up into the clouds to meet the Lord in the air. The church will be eternally displayed to show to all God's creations the exceeding riches of His grace (Eph. 2:7).

It is through the inspired pen of the Apostle Paul that we know the nature, purpose and form of organization of the local churches. It is through his writings that we learn the desire of the Holy Spirit concerning our conduct toward each other in the church, concerning the gathering of the offerings, and other doctrines and programs connected with the New Testament church——the body of Christ.

It is through the inspired pen of Paul that we learn we shall not all die, but that some of the members of the body of Christ will escape death by being caught up to meet the Lord in the air (I Thess. 4:13—18). It is through Paul's writings that we learn that the dead in Christ shall rise first, and that living saints will be changed in the twinkling of an eye (I Cor. 15:52; I Thess. 4:13—18). I know all of the Bible is God's Holy Word, and I know that all Scripture is given by inspiration; but I must confess that I find my greatest joy in studying the Epistles of Paul.

It was to the Apostle Paul that God revealed the unfolding doctrine of the Grace of God . . . that we are saved by God's grace through faith——(not by grace through faith plus Law, but by pure grace alone). We learn through the writings of Paul that our justification, our sanctification, our victory and finally the glory we will share with Jesus are all ours because of His sacrificial death on the cross, through which He purchased redemption, sanctification, righteousness, and glory for every believer.

Paul made it clear to all to whom he spoke and wrote, that his message was neither OF man nor BY man——but was a direct revelation from Almighty God through Jesus Christ. Paul was converted through the personal ministry of the Lord Jesus Christ as He appeared to him on the road to Damascus (Acts 9). Paul witnessed the glorified Christ. In I Corinthians 15 he mentions the individuals and the groups who saw Jesus after His resurrection, and refers to himself in these words: "After that, He was seen of James; then of all the apostles. AND LAST OF ALL HE WAS SEEN OF ME ALSO, AS OF ONE BORN OUT OF DUE TIME" (I Cor. 15:7–8). Thank God, that day as Paul traveled the road to Damascus, with blood in his eyes and murder in his heart, with a pocket full of letters giving him authority to arrest all who were "in this way" (Acts 9:2), suddenly a light from heaven shone round about him. Paul fell to the earth. He heard a voice which said to him, "Why persecutest thou me?" Paul answered, "Who art thou, Lord?" The answer came back, "I am Jesus whom thou persecutest. It is hard for thee to kick against the pricks." Upon hearing these words, Paul trembled. He was astonished. He asked, "Lord, what wilt thou have me to do?" In answer to that question the Lord Jesus said, "Arise and go into the city and it shall be told thee what thou must do." I am so glad, so thankful, that Paul did not argue, but obeyed the instruction received from the lips of the Lord Jesus.

This man who was trained in the school of Gamaliel,

a Pharisee of the Pharisees, a member of the Sanhedrin, a doctor of the Law, could have said, "I do not need to be instructed what to do. I am very capable of doing what I feel in my heart I should do." But Paul did not say that. In the voice of the Lord Jesus he recognized a power he had never experienced. Therefore, he asked the Lord Jesus what he should do, and then without argument, *he did it!* Thank God for the obedience of Paul that day on the Damascus road.

The conversion of the Apostle Paul marked the beginning of one of the greatest individuals who ever lived. So far as I am concerned, there has never been a greater one, except the man Christ Jesus. Surely God must have respected Paul very highly. By his pen Jehovah God, through the Holy Ghost, gave to us thirteen of the New Testament books. We can sum up the life of this apostle, this great spiritual giant, in the first words of the Epistle to the Romans: "Paul, a servant of Jesus Christ!"

THE HISTORICAL SETTING
OF THE EPHESIAN LETTER

For the historical background of the Ephesian letter, we must turn to the book of Acts, chapters 19 and 20. In these two chapters we learn that Paul spent three years in Ephesus——the longest time he spent in any one city or community. Ephesus was the capital of heathen worship in that day, but Paul had a great ministry there. In his Epistle, he reminds the elders in the church at Ephesus, "By the space of three years I ceased not TO WARN EVERYONE NIGHT AND DAY WITH TEARS!" Think of it! For three years (thirty-six months) Paul preached and cried out against sin and idolatry. As a result, there was a tremendous spiritual awakening. Many brought their books of magic and curious arts and burned them. They were placed in a huge pile in the city square, and burned "BEFORE ALL." (The price of the books burned was fifty thousand pieces of silver.)

Immediately following this, the Holy Spirit tells us "mightily grew the Word of God and prevailed" (Acts 19:20).

The entire city of Ephesus was stirred, moved, and alarmed because the devotees and the apostles of Diana were turning to this Gospel of Jesus Christ. The center of the worship of Diana was in the city of Ephesus. The temple of Diana was there, with the image "which fell down from Jupiter" (Acts 19:35). (That is, of course, according to the belief of the people in that day. They thought this great image fell from Jupiter down to the city of Ephesus.)

Paul's three-year revival upset the worship of the great image of Diana. Please notice when this New Testament evangelist moved into the city of Ephesus he did not run a full-page ad in the daily paper announcing that he would preach a series of sermons on the evils of Diana. He did not attack the image as such. He preached Jesus Christ——crucified, buried, risen. He lifted up the Lord Jesus, the Light of the world. He pointed the idol-worshippers to the one true God——and as a result a great revival followed.

I believe in negative preaching——but the positive must precede the negative. When people turn *to* the living God, they automatically turn *from* their idols (I Thess. 1:9). Paul pointed the Ephesian idolators to the Lamb of God, and when they saw the Christ, the great idol of Diana lost its glamor.

The temple of Diana was grand and glorious. It was magnificent beyond words. It was four hundred and twenty-five feet long, it was two hundred and twenty feet wide, and it was counted one of the wonders of the whole wide world. This magnificent temple overshadowed the whole city (and the life of everyone in the city) until the Apostle Paul arrived. Surely Paul must have been stricken with deep grief when he saw the people fall down and worship the heathen goddess Diana. Can you not hear the people cry out, "Can you present to us a greater god, a greater temple, than our god and our temple?" and Paul's answer, "My God can certainly boast of a finer temple, and my Christ—living in the Heavenlies— is much greater than Diana!" Paul offered to the idolators at Ephesus the message which claimed that the followers of Jesus are *"blessed with all spiritual blessings in heavenly places in Christ"* (Eph. 1:3).

The Holy Ghost had revealed to the Apostle Paul that believers are members of the body of Christ, the heavenly temple, certainly surpassing any and all earthly temples. The temple of God, the New Testament church, is glorious, a holy temple, without spot or wrinkle or any such thing (Eph. 2:21, Eph. 5:27). Paul held up before the idolators at Ephesus, the body of Christ, made up of born again blood washed individuals who embrace grace by faith, purchased at the tremendous price of the cross. The power of the Gospel preached three years night and day with tears broke down the stronghold of idolatry and brought about a revival which swept the great city of Ephesus.

Do not think, dear reader, that you can gather the hidden riches of this Epistle by simply reading the words penned down by Paul. To receive the spiritual blessings, the spiritual depth that is in this Epistle, requires the mind of the Spirit. Paul warns, "The natural man receiveth not the things of the Spirit of God: for they are foolishness unto him: neither can he know them, because they are spiritually discerned" (I Cor. 2:14). Therefore, we must have THE SPIRIT WHICH IS OF GOD if we would KNOW THE THINGS THAT ARE FREELY GIVEN TO US OF GOD, the things which THE HOLY GHOST TEACHES, COMPARING SPIRITUAL THINGS WITH SPIRITUAL (I Cor. 2:12–13). There is no part of holy Scripture that contains deeper spiritual truth than these short chapters we are about to study; therefore, it is necessary to make sure that you have the mind of the Spirit as you begin to read and study this Epistle.

To all believers who will approach the Epistle in the attitude of humility, wholeheartedly yielding to the Spirit, trusting in Him who is able to give wisdom and understanding, completely relying upon Him who is able to quicken the mind, open the eyes and enlighten the heart (Eph. 1:18), to that believer Ephesians will become a gold mine of spiritual truth, and a spring of living water in the middle of a great desert. If we approach this Epistle with fear and trembling, with humility and sincerity, He who dictated these words to the Apostle Paul will enrich our lives and bless our hearts, making us vessels meet for the Master's use. May God use this study to enrich your life and cause you to become a stronger Christian, is my prayer.

O. B. G.

CONTENTS

CONTENTS

1. Paul, an apostle of Jesus Christ by the will of God, to the saints which are at Ephesus, and to the faithful in Christ Jesus:

2. Grace be to you, and peace, from God our Father, and from the Lord Jesus Christ.

3. Blessed be the God and Father of our Lord Jesus Christ, who hath blessed us with all spiritual blessings in heavenly places in Christ:

4. According as he hath chosen us in him before the foundation of the world, that we should be holy and without blame before him in love:

5. Having predestinated us unto the adoption of children by Jesus Christ to himself, according to the good pleasure of his will,

6. To the praise of the glory of his grace, wherein he hath made us accepted in the beloved.

7. In whom we have redemption through his blood, the forgiveness of sins, according to the riches of his grace;

8. Wherein he hath abounded toward us in all wisdom and prudence;

9. Having made known unto us the mystery of his will, according to his good pleasure which he hath purposed in himself:

10. That in the dispensation of the fulness of times he might gather together in one all things in Christ, both which are in heaven, and which are on earth; even in him:

11. In whom also we have obtained an inheritance, being predestinated according to the purpose of him who worketh all things after the counsel of his own will:

12. That we should be to the praise of his glory, who first trusted in Christ.

13. In whom ye also trusted, after that ye heard the word of truth, the gospel of your salvation: in whom also after that ye believed, ye were sealed with that holy Spirit of promise,

14. Which is the earnest of our inheritance until the redemption of the purchased possession, unto the praise of his glory.

15. Wherefore I also, after I heard of your faith in the Lord Jesus, and love unto all the saints,

16. Cease not to give thanks for you, making mention of you in my prayers;

17. That the God of our Lord Jesus Christ, the Father of glory, may give unto you the spirit of wisdom and revelation in the knowledge of him:

18. The eyes of your understanding being enlightened; that ye may know what is the hope of his calling, and what the riches of the glory of his inheritance in the saints,

19. And what is the exceeding greatness of his power to us-ward who believe, according to the working of his mighty power,

20. Which he wrought in Christ, when he raised him from the dead, and set him at his own right hand in the heavenly places,

21. Far above all principality, and power, and might, and dominion, and every name that is named, not only in this world, but also in that which is to come:

22. And hath put all things under his feet, and gave him to be the head over all things to the church,

23. Which is his body, the fulness of him that filleth all in all.

OUR STANDING AS BELIEVERS

Our standing as believers is set forth in the first chapter of Ephesians:

Verse 1: "Paul, an apostle of Jesus Christ by the will of God, to the saints which are at Ephesus, and to the faithful in Christ Jesus."

There are three things I would like to point out in this verse:

1–"Paul, an apostle of Jesus Christ by the will of God."

There is no place in the Word of God where the *will* of God is so exalted as in Ephesians, yet so wondrously linked with God's grace. Ephesians is an exposition of the sovereign will of God . . . the beginning *from* which, the end *toward* which, THE REDEMPTION OF GRACE PROCEEDS. God is sovereign––but the sovereignty of God does not destroy the free will of individuals, as we will clearly see in our study of Ephesians. Paul was an apostle––not *by* man, not *of* man, not because of the *will* of man––but by the will of God. Paul was a chosen vessel to make known the mystery hidden from the foundation of the world, but revealed to us upon whom the ends of the world have come. Knowing that he was an apostle by the sovereign will of God, Paul wanted every believer to know and be assured of the same spiritual truth. Let me repeat: The sovereign will of God and the sovereign grace of God do not destroy the free will of individuals.

2–"To the saints . . . ." *Saint* is God's name for every born again child of God. The word "saint" means

15

"holy, or set apart"; the term "saint" refers to the believer's standing in Christ, and is applied to even the most unworthy believer. For example, in I Corinthians 1:2 we find, "Unto the church of God which is at Corinth . . . called to be saints, with all that in every place call upon the name of Jesus Christ our Lord, both their's and our's." In the original language of the Bible, "to be" is not in this statement, but simply "called saints." Please notice the term *saint* is used concerning all in "the church of God which is at Corinth." If you will read the first and second letters Paul wrote to the Corinthians, you will note that some of these dear people certainly did not act like saints——but in spite of their carnality they were saints because they were born again and were members of the body of Christ. All believers are saints because all believers are "in Christ."

3—"To the faithful in Christ Jesus." "Faithful" is the description of the believer when he lives the kind of life that every saint of God should live. If we are what we should be as a believer, we will be faithful in all that we do and say and in all that we are, for Christ's sake. When it fully dawns upon us that we are God's saints, the fact of sainthood will cause us to want to be faithful servants of the God who provided sovereign grace that we as individuals might be born again. We are saints ——and we should be faithful because we are *in Christ Jesus*:

In Colossians 1:27 Paul declares, ". . . Christ in you, the hope of glory." Again, "There is therefore now no condemnation to them which are in Christ Jesus" (Rom. 8:1).

Again, "For ye are dead, and your life is hid with Christ in God" (Col. 3:3).

"Therefore if any man be in Christ, he is a new

creature" (II Cor. 5:17). Notice in all of these Scriptures we are declared to be "in Christ" if we are children of God.

Someone may be asking, "How do we get *in Christ*?" Our Textbook gives us the answer:

"For as the body is one, and hath many members, and all the members of that one body, being many, are one body: *so also is Christ*. For by one Spirit are we all baptized into one body, whether we be Jews or Gentiles, whether we be bond or free; and have been all made to drink into one Spirit" (I Cor. 12:12–13).

We become a member of the body of Christ——bone of His bone, flesh of His flesh (Eph. 5:30) through the baptism of the Holy Ghost; and this occurs the instant, the split second, we believe on the Lord Jesus Christ as our personal Saviour. Jesus declares, "Except a man be born of the Spirit he cannot enter the kingdom of God" (John 3:5). The spiritual birth through the power of God is an imperative if we would enter the kingdom of God. We are *saints* because we are in Christ Jesus. All believers should be *faithful because* we are saints in Christ Jesus.

Verse 2: "Grace be to you, and peace, from God our Father, and from the Lord Jesus Christ."

Paul was a Grace preacher. To this chosen vessel of God, by the sovereign will of God it was revealed that by Grace through Faith, hell-deserving sinners become sons and saints in Jesus Christ. Notice Paul says, "*Grace* be to you . . . and *peace*." The Holy Spirit is very careful in the Word of God to place every word in its right position. Paul did not say "Peace and grace," because apart from the *grace of God* there is no peace *with* God. When we become the recipients of God's grace,

17

then we have peace that passes all understanding; but apart from God's grace there is no peace . . . there can be no peace. The statement "from God our Father and the Lord Jesus Christ" is not just a tribute to the deity of the Son who is co-equal with God the Father. The statement sets before us the exalted position of Jesus with the Father "in the heavenlies." This position is set forth and unfolded by the Holy Spirit throughout the Ephesian letter.

Please note that Grace and Peace are in Christ Jesus. There is no other place to find grace. "In the beginning was the Word, and the Word was with God, and the Word was God . . . And the Word was made flesh, and dwelt among us, (and we beheld His glory, the glory as of the only begotten of the Father,) FULL OF GRACE and truth" (John 1:1 and 14).

Jesus was in the beginning with the Father, in the bosom of the Father (John 1:18).

Jesus took a body——He was God in flesh (II Cor. 5:19).

Jesus took a body of flesh for a specific and singular purpose: "That He by the grace of God should taste death for every man" (Heb. 2:9).

Therefore, all spiritual blessings come through the grace of God in Christ Jesus.

THE BELIEVER'S POSITION IN THE GRACE OF GOD

Verse 3: "Blessed be the God and Father of our Lord Jesus Christ, who hath blessed us with all spiritual blessings in heavenly places in Christ."

The statement *"in Christ Jesus"* (or the same statement expressed in other words) appears fourteen times

18

in the first chapter of Ephesians. "In Christ Jesus" is the key that unlocks this storehouse of spiritual blessings. "In Christ Jesus" is the key that opens the door and permits us to look into the storehouse of this Epistle. Every believer, every born again child of God is "in Christ Jesus" because he has been baptized by the Holy Spirit into the body of Christ (I Cor. 12:12–13). Because we are *in* Christ Jesus we share all heaven's spiritual blessings *with* Christ Jesus. Paul makes the same statement in other words in Philippians 4:19: "But my God shall supply all your need according to his riches in glory *in Christ Jesus*."

In the eighth chapter of Romans we learn that we are the children of God. We have the witness of the Holy Spirit that we are the children of God, and because we are His children we are heirs of God and joint-heirs with the Lord Jesus, our Saviour (Rom. 8:4–17).

What God's storehouse contains *in Christ Jesus*, only eternity will reveal. Certainly the finite mind of man cannot conceive of the spiritual blessings (and the physical blessings) contained in God's mighty storehouse––but it is only in Christ Jesus that we can claim these supplies as we need them, spiritually and physically. What is ours "in Christ Jesus" now? What is our present standing, our present riches, our present power, is known only in part. We know we are the children of God, we know He can supply our need. We know He will never leave us nor forsake us––but these finite minds and our limited faith cannot conceive the fullness of the blessing that rests upon us now as we sit together in heavenly places in Christ Jesus.

Verse 4: "According as He hath chosen us in Him before the foundation of the world, that we should be holy and without blame before Him in love."

In the original language of the Bible, Ephesians 1: 3–14 is one sentence . . . the longest sentence in the Word of God. There is a reason for this: Into these verses is woven the most thrilling account of spiritual blessings and provisions revealed in the Word of God. There is no place for a period in this account, because *three Persons* are involved. They are inseparable, both in their being and in their activity as having to do with our salvation. Therefore, Ephesians 1:3–14 is one great sentence, describing the one great provision made for hell-deserving sinners.

Referring back to verse 3 for just a moment, we note the verse opens with "Blessed," which means literally, "well spoken of." Certainly as we think of the gracious wonders and the indescribable love that made possible for us the redemption provided by God our Father, we must of necessity speak well of God who so loved us that He gave His only begotten Son that we (hell-deserving sinners) might be saved. In our testimonies we thank the Lord Jesus for saving us, and we thank the Holy Spirit for leading us. Certainly Jesus is to be thanked for saving us, and the Holy Spirit is to be praised; but Paul adds "And not only so, but we also joy in God through our Lord Jesus Christ, by whom we have now received the atonement" (Rom. 5:11).

It is true that Jesus died on the cross, and we have redemption through His blood. It is in Christ Jesus that we rest, saved by His grace. But never forget it was God the Father who so loved sinners that He by His grace (Heb. 2:9) permitted Jesus to die the horrible, indescribable death He died that we might be saved!

The virgin birth is clearly taught in verse 3 of our present chapter. God IS the God and the Father of our Lord Jesus Christ, despite what some of the modern bishops and "religious fathers" have had to say about Jesus being just an ordinary man. He was born of a virgin—but God Almighty was His Father, and the blood of Almighty God ran through the veins of Jesus (Acts 20:28).

God the Father, God the Son, and God the Spirit are all three in these verses. Their work is unfolded in verses 4 through 14 of chapter one. God the Father planned and was the Originator of every spiritual blessing. All spiritual blessings are ours (if we are believers) *in Christ*, by Whom we were redeemed. All spiritual blessings are Spirit-bestowed. God's blessings in the Spirit come only as we yield fully to the leadership of the Holy Spirit. If we refuse to be led *by* the Spirit, we cannot hope to share the blessings *of* the Spirit.

The statement "in the heavenlies" is used five times in the Ephesian letter. It is found only one other time in the Scriptures. Jesus said, "If I have told you earthly things, and ye believe not, how shall ye believe, if I tell you OF HEAVENLY THINGS?" (John 3:12). Here Jesus was instructing a very religious Pharisee who needed to be born from above.

The origin of all spiritual blessings is "in the heavenlies." Why?

Because our Heavenly Father is in the heavenlies (Matt. 7:11).

From there our Saviour came (John 6:33).

The Holy Spirit came from the heavenlies (Acts 2:2—4).

Above all other reasons, the Lord Jesus Christ is there *now!* When He had by Himself purged our sins, He ascended back to the Father, sat down on the right hand of the Majesty, and He is there today to make intercession for us (Heb. 1:1–3).

"For there is one God, and one Mediator between God and men, the man Christ Jesus" (I Tim. 2:5).

Jesus the man——not the Spirit, not a mystic——but THE MAN, is in heaven *now*, seated *now* on the right hand of God the Father, interceding and mediating for all saints in Christ Jesus.

If we are born again, our spiritual life is "in Him" (I John 5:11). Therefore, every spiritual blessing comes through HIM.

Believers are strangers and pilgrims on this earth. This is not our home. Our citizenship is in heaven. Believers are identified with Christ:

(a) In nature (II Peter 1:4).
(b) In life (Col. 3:4; I John 5:12).
(c) In relationship (John 20:17; Heb. 2:11).
(d) In service (John 17:18; Matt. 28:20).
(e) In suffering (Phil. 1:29; Rom. 8:17; Col. 1:24).
(f) In inheritance (Rom. 8:16–17).
(g) In future glory (Rom. 8:18–21; I Peter 2:9; Rev. 1:6; Rev. 5:10).

Born again believers are heavenly citizens. We are a heavenly people, we are definitely strangers on this earth (Heb. 3:1; I Peter 2:11).

The Lord Jesus Christ, our Saviour, has been victorious——not only on earth, but in the heavenlies. He conquered the world, the flesh, and the devil, death, hell and the grave. He has the key to death and hell. "ALL POWER IS GIVEN UNTO ME IN HEAVEN AND IN EARTH!" (Matt. 28:18). Today Jesus is in heaven. Today Jesus is exercising Himself in our behalf, supplying our needs while we remain on earth. In John 17 Jesus prayed, making it clear that He was not asking the Heavenly Father to take us out of the earth, but to take care of us while we remain on earth.

There is a tremendous spiritual truth that needs to be learned by many professing Christians. Some are born again, while others are deceived. The truth to which I refer is set forth in I John 4:4:

"Ye are of God, little children, and have overcome them: because greater is He that is in you, than he that is in the world."

Were it not for the fact that Jesus lives today, seated at the right hand of the Father to intercede for us, spiritual life on this earth would be an impossibility. We live in a non-spiritual atmosphere. We live in a world that is steeped in sin. The whole world "lieth in the lap of the wicked one." Therefore, if we were not literally connected to the heavenly Man who makes intercession for us and pleads our case before a holy God, it would be impossible for us to live a spiritual life on this earth. In Him "we live and move and have our being." In Christ we have salvation. In Christ we have strength to live a Christian life. In Christ we overcome Satan. In Christ our needs are all supplied.

Divers go below the surface of the ocean; but they carry air with them. Man cannot live under water except he be supplied with air from earth. Thus, man born of God cannot live a spiritual life without a constant supply of Heaven-sent grace, strength, power and blessing. The song-writer expresses it in these words:

> *"Moment by moment I'm kept in His love,*
> *Moment by moment I've life from above."*

Yes, we could say, "second by second," and then break it down to "split-second by split-second we have life from above"——because if Jesus withdrew His power and His grace for one split second, we could not stand . . . we surely would fall! I am so glad "if God be for us, who can be against us?" (Rom. 8:31).

The term "all spiritual blessing" does not mean just spiritual blessings——but literally means "Spirit-bestowed blessings." The grace of God provides our every need. There is no need too small or too insignificant for the Heavenly Father to see. His concern reaches our utmost need. God's love assures us that He will, through Jesus, "FREELY GIVE US ALL THINGS" (Rom. 8:32). God's promise is "EVERY NEED SUPPLIED" (Phil. 4:19).

It pleased God the Father to reveal to Paul (through the Holy Ghost) that all believers are saints . . . saints because all believers are *in Christ* (Col. 1:27; Col. 3:3). Christ was once dead but is now alive, was once on this earth but is now seated at the right hand of God the Father in the heavenlies——(not only in *Heaven*, but in "the heavenlies"). To be *in Christ* includes all spiritual riches, all spiritual realities; and in Him is revealed all blessings afforded by the marvelous grace of God.

The only way any man can please God is *in Christ Jesus.* God the Father has highly exalted His Son, and in the Son God is highly pleased. The reason? Jesus came into this world with a single eye, a single desire, a single motive, to do the sovereign will of God the Father. Therefore, God saves us for Christ's sake (Eph. 4:32). God blesses us with all spiritual blessings in Christ Jesus, and ONLY in Christ Jesus. If you ever hear God the Father say, "Well done, good and faithful servant," it will only be because you stand before God *in Christ Jesus.*

There is no pastor, minister, evangelist, teacher, preacher, priest, or pope who can confess you to God

24

the Father! The one Mediator, the man Christ Jesus, must confess you to the Heavenly Father (I Tim. 2:5, I John 2:1–2, Matt. 10:31ff). So, my precious reader, if you are not in Christ Jesus you are hopelessly lost and entirely cut off from God the Father! Jesus is the Alpha and the Omega. He is the first and the last. He is the Author and the Finisher of our faith. He is the door to Heaven——and in His own words, "No man cometh unto the Father but by me!" (John 14:6).

Jesus is our Saviour. We are crucified with Christ (Gal. 2:20).

We are resurrected to walk in newness of life (Rom. 6:1ff).

We walk in newness of life because we are a new creation in Christ (II Cor. 5:17).

Our access to God the Father in prayer is through the Lord Jesus Christ (Rom. 8:26–27).

Our strength for service is in the Lord Jesus Christ (Acts 17:28 and Heb. 13:8).

Our sufficiency in the hour of trial is in the Lord Jesus (I Peter 1:3–9).

Our future glory is in the Lord Jesus Christ——and if we suffer with Him we will reign with Him; but if we deny Him He will also deny us (Rom. 8:17).

In the Lord Jesus Christ ". . . the world, or life, or death, or things present, or things to come; ALL ARE YOUR'S; and ye are Christ's; and Christ is God's" (I Cor. 3:22–23). After reading such a statement, who could keep from saying, "Hallelujah! What a Saviour!"

THE TRINITY
AND THE PART OF EACH MEMBER OF THE GODHEAD IN OUR CHRISTIAN EXPERIENCE

Some dear Christian people (yes, even born again people) think of the Trinity only as connected with the study of theology. There are many pros and cons concerning the Trinity. Some declare that the doctrine originated in the Roman Catholic church——which, of course, is false. The Trinity was in the beginning——God the Father, God the Son, God the Holy Ghost:

Genesis 1:1: "In the beginning . . . God." There is *God the Father.*

John 1:1-3: "In the beginning was the Word, and the Word was with God, and the Word was God. The same was in the beginning with God. ALL THINGS WERE MADE BY HIM; and without Him was not any thing made that was made." And in John 1:14 the Holy Ghost enlightens us as to who the Word is:

"And the Word was made flesh, and dwelt among us, (and we beheld His glory, the glory as of the only begotten of the Father,) full of grace and truth." *The Word is Jesus.*

In the beginning, God the Father created all things by God the Son.——For some reason upon which we will not speculate here, judgment struck the earth, and "the earth was without form, and void." But in Genesis 1:2 we see the Third Person of the Godhead: ". . . and the *Spirit of God* moved upon the face of the waters."

Therefore, in Genesis 1:1-2 we have the doctrine of the Trinity. But we are not to think of the Trinity as a theological fact only. Each member of the Godhead has a definite part in our salvation. If you are redeemed, if you are in Christ Jesus, rejoicing with joy unspeakable and full of glory . . . it is because of what *God the Father* has done, plus what *God the Son* has done, plus what *God the Spirit* has done.

God the Father so loved us that He yielded up His only begotten Son, that we (hell-deserving sinners) might be saved (John 3:16–18).

God the Son left the bosom of the Father (John 1:18), took a body (Rom. 8:1–3) and in that body Jesus tasted death for every man (Heb. 2:9). He was crucified and buried——but death could not hold Him. He rose again for our justification (Rom. 5:1–13, I Cor. 15:1–5). Now Jesus, our High Priest, is in heaven, in the heavenly tabernacle, pleading for us. Christ our High Priest accomplished the atonement on Calvary, carried the blood of the atonement into the holy of holies——not into the temple here on this earth, but into very heaven itself. Jesus presented the blood to the Father, and the Father accepted it. Therefore we have redemption through His blood:

"For Christ is not entered into the holy places made with hands, which are the figures of the true; but into heaven itself, now to appear in the presence of God for us" (Heb. 9:24).

In the Old Testament era, the high priest appointed by Jehovah God entered into the holy of holies in the tabernacle, an acting representative for the people of God . . . for *all* the people . . . bearing upon his shoulders the names of the twelve tribes engraven on the precious stones of his breastplate. Thus in the person of the high priest the people of God were carried into the very presence of God Himself. In the same way now, in the person of Jesus Christ, we who are born again and united to Him through the miracle of the Holy Ghost, are represented by Him and accepted as holy and without blemish before

Him . . . in the presence of Almighty God (Eph. 1:4). In Jesus, our High Priest, we are not only presented before God, but we are made to sit together in Christ in the heavenlies (Eph. 2:6).

In the tabernacle in the Old Testament, there was found only one piece of furniture——the ark——typifying our Lord Jesus Christ in His deity and also in His humanity. In the ark was found the Law (the Law broken by man—— but perfectly kept in Jesus). Also in the ark was the manna (an omer full——the daily portion for one man, enough for his day by day needs). In Jesus, our day by day need, our daily portion is met.

Also in the ark was Aaron's rod that budded, typically teaching that Christ, through His resurrection, has been forever established in His high priestly position. He is the first fruits of them that slept. On the very day of His resurrection He called His followers (us) "brethren." Jesus is now gone into the heavenlies, thereby pledging that one day He will return to "bring many sons into glory" (Heb. 2:10).

Upon the ark was found the mercy seat. Over the mercy seat was the blood of the atonement, and the overshadowing, living presence of the cherubim. The blood covers the broken Law, changing the throne of this universe from a judgment seat to a mercy seat for this glorious age of the Grace of God.

There is one further feature of the ark that I would like to point out in connection with our study and the spiritual teaching of Ephesians: *The staves*. The staves were "not to be taken from it." By the staves the ark was carried in the midst of God's people as they journeyed. It was present in all of their journeyings. While the ark was in the glory room, the holy of holies, it set forth the standing of the people of God. (Compare Eph.

28

1:1-3.) But the ark was also designed to be moved so that it was continually with the people as they journeyed (read Eph. 1:4-6). Therefore the ark is a type of the Lord Jesus as He walks with us, never to leave us nor forsake us, that we may boldly say, "God is my helper, and I shall not fear." Since God be for us, who can be against us? God who delivered up His only Son, will by and through that Son freely give us all things. The ark ––and all having to do with the ark––sets forth a beautiful picture of the Lord Jesus, our High Priest, our Ark, the One who makes us sons of God, secure "in Christ."

In these verses we see our standing in the Lord Jesus Christ:

(a) We are chosen in Christ.

(b) We are sanctified in Christ.

(c) We are foreordained in Christ.

(d) We are adopted in Christ.

(e) We are accepted in Christ.

(f) We are redeemed in Christ.

(g) We are forgiven in Christ.

(h) We are enriched in Christ.

(i) We are enlightened in Christ, the Light of the world.

(j) Our inheritance is in Christ.

(k) We are sealed until the day of redemption in Christ (Eph. 1:13, Eph. 4:30).

Verse 4: "According as He (God) hath chosen us in Him before the foundation of the world . . . ." God the Father planned our redemption long before we were born on this earth. We who are born again were "chosen in Him" in the eternity behind us. Greek scholars tell us that the literal meaning is "chose us for Himself" . . . that is, God chose us for His own joy and pleasure and

29

glory.

Never entertain the idea that I am a hyper-Calvinist. I believe in the sovereignty of God——God knows the end from the beginning——but that has nothing to do with the free will of man. I believe in Bible election, Bible pre-destination; so do not hastily jump to any conclusions because of the statement I have just made. I am not a fatalist; I do not believe that some are elected to go to heaven while others are elected to be damned. I do not believe some are chosen to be saved, while in the mind of God, in the eternity behind us, He chose some to be damned. That is not the God I know, nor is it the Gospel I find in Ephesians.

When did God choose us? *"Before the foundation of the world."* God has a plan, He has a blueprint——and all hell cannot stop the program of Almighty God!

In Acts 15 we are told of an outstanding council at Jerusalem concerning the question of circumcision and the teaching of the legalizers from Judaea. Paul and Barnabas were there, and they had quite a discussion. When that discussion was finished, when Paul and Barnabas had testified concerning salvation of the Gentiles through the Gospel, James spoke:

"Men and brethren, hearken unto me: Simeon hath declared how God at the first did visit the Gentiles, to take out of them a people for His name. And to this agree the words of the prophets; as it is written, After this I will return, and will build again the tabernacle of David, which is fallen down; and I will build again the ruins thereof, and I will set it up: That the residue of men might seek after the Lord, and all the Gentiles, upon whom my name is called, saith the Lord, WHO DOETH ALL THESE THINGS. KNOWN UNTO GOD ARE ALL HIS WORKS FROM THE BEGINNING OF THE WORLD"

(Acts 15:14—18).

God knows the end in the beginning. Because God is sovereign, omniscient, and omnipresent, He knew in the beginning that I would be saved. God knew that I would be a part of the body of Christ; but the foreknowledge of God had nothing to do with my own free will. God did not force me to believe on the Lord Jesus Christ. I *willingly accepted Christ* as my personal Saviour. Dear friend, if you ever step inside the pearly gates it will be because you received Jesus Christ (John 1:12).

To His own people, Israel, Jesus said, "Search the Scriptures; in them ye think ye have eternal life: and they are they which testify of me." (The Jews searched the Law, they read the prophets, they sang the Psalms . . . but they refused to see the Lamb of God, the "plant out of dry ground," the humble Jesus. They searched the Scriptures——but they had their own minds made up and they refused to see Jesus *in* the Scriptures.) "AND YE WILL NOT COME TO ME, THAT YE MIGHT HAVE LIFE" (John 5:39—40).

Again, Jesus sat on the hillsides of Judaea and wept. He said to His own people Israel, God's chosen nation in the Old Testament era, "O Jerusalem, Jerusalem, which killest the prophets, and stonest them that are sent unto thee; HOW OFTEN WOULD I HAVE GATHERED THY CHILDREN TOGETHER, AS A HEN DOTH GATHER HER BROOD UNDER HER WINGS, AND YE WOULD NOT! Behold, your house is left unto you desolate: and verily I say unto you, Ye shall not see me, until the time come when ye shall say, Blessed is he that cometh in the name of the Lord" (Luke 13:34—35).

Jesus said to the Jews, "Ye will not come to me that ye might have life." To His own dear people He said, "I would have gathered your children as a hen

31

gathereth her chickens under her wings——but you would not let me!" I wonder how the hyper-Calvinist explains that away? Of course, they have their man-made explanation; but I say to you who read these lines, if you are not saved, if you go to hell when you die, it will not be God's will. It is not God's will that any perish, but that all come to repentance. And if you die in sin and go to hell it will not be because you were elected or chosen (or predestined) to be damned; it will be because you refused to come unto the Lord Jesus Christ for salvation. If you have been led astray by hyper-Calvinism, may God help you to believe on the Lord Jesus Christ this moment. Trust Him as your Saviour, receive Him by faith——and I guarantee on the authority of God's Word, God will save you for Jesus' sake, this very moment.

As I pointed out in Acts 15, God does not operate in a hit-or-miss manner. God completed His plan of the ages before He created this earth. The church as a body, a complete body without spot or wrinkle, was chosen by God *in Christ* before God created Adam. *The church* is predestined to be completed without spot or wrinkle or any such thing. *Individuals* receive or reject Jesus according to their own free will. God did not create man as a puppet or as a mechanical thing . . . an electronic brain that operates when God pushes the switch. Man is created in the image of God. Man is created with a will to choose or to reject the way of righteousness. I am so glad God placed Adam and Eve in a garden, and gave to them the right to choose. I am glad the tree of the knowledge of good and evil was placed in the Garden. Adam was clearly instructed by God as to what he could do, and what he was not to do. I am glad God gave Adam the right and the opportunity to choose. God, in Christ, has done for man what man could never have done for himself.

32

Be sure to weigh this next statement before you reject it: God in Christ has done for man what man *would not* have done for himself if he could have! Man is totally and entirely depraved, but in Christ we are just as just as Jesus our Justifier is just (Rom. 5:1ff). In the sight of God we are just as pure and holy as the blood of the Lord Jesus that covers our sins. We as individuals have to do with Christ our Saviour——our High Priest, our Mediator. God has committed into the hands of Jesus all authority in heaven and on earth, and we have to do with Christ. He is the One who saves us, leads us, keeps us——and He is the One who will present us to the Father. I repeat: The church as an organism, a body of which Jesus is the head and the foundation (Eph. 5 and I Cor. 3) was elected, chosen, and predestined by God before the foundation of this world.

We, as individuals, are in Christ because we have believed in His finished work. God's act of choosing us before the foundation of the world was "in Christ" the Son. Before the beginning of things as we know earthly things today, Jesus had already given Himself over to the Father in solemn covenant for the work of redemption. He (Jesus) ". . . the Lamb slain from the foundation of the world" (Rev. 13:8) willingly laid His life down that we might have life. The blood of Jesus Christ was declared to be the only way of salvation before God ever made the earth or man.

"But as He which hath called you is holy, so be ye holy in all manner of conversation; because it is written, Be ye holy; for I am holy. And if ye call on the Father, who WITHOUT RESPECT OF PERSONS judgeth according to every man's work, pass the time of your sojourning here in fear: Forasmuch as ye know that ye are not redeemed with corruptible things, as silver and gold, from your vain conversation received by tradition from your fathers; BUT WITH THE PRECIOUS BLOOD OF CHRIST, AS OF A LAMB WITHOUT BLEMISH AND WITHOUT SPOT: WHO VERILY WAS FOREORDAINED BEFORE THE FOUNDATION OF THE WORLD, BUT WAS MANIFEST IN THESE LAST TIMES FOR YOU. Who by Him do believe in God, that raised Him up from the dead, and gave Him glory; that your faith and hope might be in God. Seeing ye have purified your souls in obeying the truth through the Spirit unto unfeigned love of the brethren, see that ye love one another with a pure heart fervently: being born again, not of corruptible seed, but of incorruptible, by the Word of God, which liveth and abideth forever" (I Peter 1:15–23).

In these verses we learn that the blood of Jesus was foreordained before God ever made this universe. The redemption price of a soul is the blood——nothing less. God demands blood . . . the blood of an innocent, sinless sacrifice——and that could have been no one except the Son. So——it was agreed between Father and Son that Jesus would die on the cross for the remission of sin. This covenant was made between the members of the Godhead before God ever created this universe or anything therein.

Why did God choose us? What was the purpose of His choosing? Did God choose us just to save us——or for something far greater? The answer is, God chose us ". . . THAT WE SHOULD BE HOLY AND WITHOUT BLAME IN HIS PRESENCE."

Jesus expresses the same truth in these words: "Ye have not chosen Me, but I have chosen you, and ordained you, that ye should go and bring forth fruit . . ." (John 15:16a).

To the believers at Thessalonica Paul said: "But we are bound to give thanks alway to God for you, brethren beloved of the Lord, because God hath from the beginning chosen you to salvation through sanctification of the Spirit and belief of the truth: Whereunto He called you by our Gospel, to the obtaining of the glory of our Lord Jesus Christ" (II Thess. 2:13—14).

To the believers in Rome Paul said: "For whom He did foreknow, He also did predestinate to be conformed to the image of His Son, that He might be the firstborn among many brethren. Moreover whom He did predestinate, them He also called: and whom He called, them He also justified: and whom He justified, them He also glorified. What shall we then say to these things? If God be for us, who can be against us? He that spared not His own Son, but delivered Him up for us all, how shall He not with Him also freely give us all things?" (Rom. 8:29—32). Every born again, blood washed, redeemed child of God is predestined to be conformed to the image of the Son of God, "without spot or wrinkle or any such thing."

Election, predestination, and the foreknowledge of God is to be taught to spiritually-minded believers—— *never* to be preached to unbelievers in a mixed multitude. God pity the preacher who will stand before an audience made up of believers and unbelievers, and preach to that mixed audience that some are elected to be saved, and if they are elected they will be saved; but if they are not elected they cannot be saved. God pity such stupid spiritual ignorance!

Verse 5: "Having predestinated us unto the adoption of children by Jesus Christ to Himself, according to the good pleasure of His will."

Predestination is the bringing to pass of things determined by God in the eternity behind us. Every believer is predestined to be conformed to the image of the Son of God. Conformation occurs as we walk in the Spirit, feeding upon the milk and the meat of the Word. When we are born again we are babes in Christ. We are commanded to desire the sincere milk of the Word that we may grow, and it is God's good pleasure that we become strong in the Lord, good soldiers, fully grown spiritual men and women in Christ. We are to work out our own salvation with fear and trembling. We do not work FOR our salvation . . . salvation is God's gift; but after receiving salvation we are to work out our own salvation with fear and trembling. We are to grow and become stronger day by day, as we study and feed upon the bread, meat, and milk of the Word of the living God.

In verse 5 the word *adoption* has to do with our position, not with our relationship to God. Every believer is a son of God, a child of God through the new birth. We are born——not of blood nor of the will of the flesh nor of the will of man——but "born of God" (John 1:12–13). We are adopted into the family of God through the act of God, placing us in the position of an adult son. Study carefully Galatians 4:1–5 and you will see what I mean.

This may be a poor illustration, but perhaps it will help someone to see what I am trying to get across. We become a son of God, a babe in Christ, through the miracle of the new birth. We are born of the Holy Spirit (John 3:5). Under the Law, a babe was under tutors until it reached a certain age. When the child became of age, he became *heir*. Thank God, under grace we are not only born sons of God, but we are adopted into the family of God, giving to us the position of heirship. The minute we are born again we become an heir of God and a joint-heir with Jesus Christ (Rom. 8:17). We are not under the Law, we are under Grace. We are not under instructors, but the Grace of God teaches us (Titus 2:11–15). We are predestinated and adopted children of God in Christ, who is the firstborn among many brethren. Christ satisfied the heart of God in every minute detail, fulfilled the Law and the prophets——every jot and every tittle (Matt. 5:17—18), completed the work the Father gave Him to do (John 17) and when He had Himself purged our sins He sat down on the right hand of the Majesty on high (Heb. 1:1—3).

Verse 6: "To the praise of the glory of His grace, wherein He hath made us accepted in the beloved."

We are now accepted by God the Father——*in the Beloved*, the Son. When Jesus was baptized God said, "This is my beloved Son in whom I am well pleased." On the Mount of Transfiguration God said concerning Jesus, "This is my beloved Son in whom I am well pleased. Hear ye Him!"

Just before Jesus began walking the last mile of the way to Calvary He cried out, "What shall I say? Shall I say, Father, save me from this hour?" Then He answered immediately, "No! I came into the world for this hour! Father, glorify thy name!"

"Then came there a voice from Heaven, saying, I HAVE BOTH GLORIFIED IT, AND WILL GLORIFY IT AGAIN! The people therefore, that stood by, and heard it, said that it thundered: others said an angel spake to Him. Jesus answered and said, This voice came not because of me, but for your sakes" (John 12:23—30).

We are accepted by God the Father because we have received the Saviour, the Son. What assurance we have, beloved! We are sons of God, children of God, adopted into the family of God, thereby an heir of God . . . accepted by God in the beloved, the Lord Jesus Christ who is our High Priest. Therefore we, as sons, come boldly to the Father in prayer, in the name of Jesus, making known our needs. Study carefully Hebrews 10:19—23.

Jesus one glorious day, will . . . "PRESENT US

FAULTLESS BEFORE THE PRESENCE OF HIS GLORY
WITH EXCEEDING JOY!" (Jude 24).

Dear sinner saved by Grace, never forget that God
has saved you for Christ's sake. God has forgiven you
for Christ's sake. God has redeemed you for Christ's
sake (Eph. 4:32). God has saved you—"*to the praise
of His glorious grace*" (Eph. 1:6). God through His great
love and His great Grace provided Jesus in a body, that
in the body of flesh Jesus might fulfill every jot and
every tittle of God's holy Law, and through His shed
blood might purchase redemption for sinners. All of this
was blueprinted, planned, purchased and provided by God
the Father in order that His Grace in Jesus might be published in all Heaven's glory. That is exactly what will
happen after the Rapture. In the consummation of all
things God will display the church (the body of Christ,
the redeemed) in the heavenlies—and all of God's creations will witness, in the church, the exceeding riches
of God's Grace (Eph. 2:6–7). "When He shall come to
be glorified in His saints, and to be admired in all them
that believe" (II Thess. 1:10).

I believe in Bible election. We need not close our
eyes and deny the doctrine of election in Scriptures. I
do not profess to fully understand election as taught in
the Scriptures, but after many years of studying the Word
of God I do feel that I understand it a little better than
I ever have before. As I have said before, election always concerns *God's people only*.

Jesus came into the world to seek and to save the
lost (Luke 19:10). The lost do not seek Jesus. The
natural man is blind, dead, totally and entirely depraved.
Something must happen from without to stir the natural
man within, before the natural man will accept Jesus as
Saviour. According to John 15:16, we who are believers

did not choose Jesus——He chose us. But remember, election never applies to anyone except believers. All others are excluded. Men are not elected to be separated from God eternally. Men are not elected to be damned. The word "election" cannot be used in such a manner. If we ever understand the election of God, we must see clearly that Christ is the first CHOSEN ONE. Christ is the first to be elect of God.

"Behold my servant, whom I uphold; mine elect (note: MINE ELECT), in whom my soul delighteth; I have put my spirit upon Him: He shall bring forth judgment to the Gentiles. He shall not cry, nor lift up, nor cause His voice to be heard in the street. A bruised reed shall He not break, and the smoking flax shall He not quench: He shall bring forth judgment unto truth. He shall not fail nor be discouraged, till He have set judgment in the earth: and the isles shall wait for His law. Thus saith God the Lord, He that created the heavens, and stretched them out; He that spread forth the earth, and that which cometh out of it; He that giveth breath unto the people upon it, and spirit to them that walk therein: I the Lord have called thee in righteousness, and will hold thine hand, and will keep thee, and give thee for a covenant of the people, for a light of the Gentiles; to open the blind eyes, to bring out the prisoners from the prison, and them that sit in darkness out of the prison house" (Isaiah 42:1–7).

From this we clearly see that Christ is the first chosen one. He is the elect of God. Then God chose US in Christ. I trust I can get across to you what I feel in my own heart and see through the eye of the inner man. God chooses us *in Jesus*. Only those who are in Jesus are accepted of God, and God has chosen everyone who will accept the Lord Jesus Christ as their personal Saviour. Let the Scriptures speak:

"Wherefore He (Jesus) is able also to save them to the uttermost that come unto God by Him, seeing He ever liveth to make intercession for them" (Heb. 7:25). God has elected a body of Christ, the New Testament church, IN Christ. God can accept the sinner only as the sinner is in Christ Jesus. God has not chosen certain individuals only to become members of the body of Christ. God loved the whole wide world; God gave Jesus for the whole wide world. Jesus died for the sins of the whole wide world. But we know—and certainly God knows—that all will not receive Jesus. But as many as receive Jesus, to them God gives the power to become sons; and when the individual receives Jesus, God "borns" that individual into the chosen body—the elect body of Christ.

Foreordination is God's enforcement act, whereby what God determined in the eternity behind us is carried out. Foreordination operates through the sovereign will of God (Eph. 1:5). Foreordination insures us that what God has purposed for all believers shall never be nullified, but shall surely come to pass. Foreordination and the free will of man, like two parallel lines that meet at infinity, harmonize in God. When we view the foreordination of God and the free will of man from eternity to eternity, we will find no conflict. Difficulties disappear and our thinking becomes clear if we will but realize that foreordination, election, predestination pertain only to God's people. Every man in the world has a free will to accept or reject Jesus Christ, every man is invited and urged to accept the Lord Jesus. He took a body of flesh and bones, that in a body like unto our body He (Jesus) ". . . by the grace of God should taste death for every man" (Heb. 2:9).

Please do not accuse the Holy Spirit of being insincere or hypocritical. If individuals are elected and predestined to be lost, if individuals are foreordained to be damned, the Holy Spirit would not have said through Paul, that Jesus by the grace of God should taste death for *every man*. On the contrary, the Holy Spirit would have said that Jesus by the grace of God came to taste death for *the elect* . . . or for *the chosen*. Please be reasonable, and face the fact that God knows the end in the beginning——yet God's knowledge of the end in the beginning has nothing to do with your free will. You as an individual have the opportunity to receive Jesus, and when you receive Jesus, God accepts you *in the Beloved*. "WHOSOEVER WILL, LET HIM TAKE OF THE WATER OF LIFE FREELY" (Rev. 22:17).

Here is the revelation the Holy Spirit has given to me concerning Bible election: God the Father elected the body——the New Testament church; and we know the body is made up of a certain number of believers. One day, some person somewhere will be born again, and that will complete the body. When the body is complete, the Rapture will take place that instant . . . "in the twinkling of an eye." God the Father elected a body. God chose a body *as a body*. The body is made up of individuals. Individuals become members of the body by receiving Jesus of their own free will.

THE SON'S PART IN OUR REDEMPTION

Verse 7: "In whom we have redemption through His blood, the forgiveness of sins, according to the riches of His grace."

God the Father *planned* our redemption (Eph. 1:4–6). God the Son actually *provided* our redemption. The last part of verse 6 clearly tells us that God accepts us *in the Beloved*——and that involves another person . . . Jesus is the *Beloved* of the Father.

Just why is Jesus "beloved"? He tells us: "Therefore doth my Father love me, because I lay down my life, that I might take it again. No man taketh it from me, but I lay it down of myself. I have power to lay it down, and I have power to take it again. This commandment have I received of my Father" (John 10:17–18). Our finite minds will never be able to grasp or understand the depth of the co-working of God the Father and God the Son in our redemption. But through the sacrifice made by the Beloved, God has "translated us into the kingdom of His dear Son" (Col. 1:13). The original Greek in that verse reads, "translated us into the kingdom of the Son of His love." The love demonstrated by God in giving His Son, the love demonstrated by the Son in freely giving Himself (the just for the unjust), will be the marvel of all eternity.

Redemption is through His blood. Jesus said, "The Son of man came not to be ministered unto, but to minister, and to give His life a ransom for many" (Matt. 20:28). In the book of Leviticus (the "Hebrews" of the Old Testament), we read, "The life is in the blood" (Lev. 17:11). Therefore, Jesus came to give His blood a ransom for many. The blood of Jesus was pure, holy, sinless, guileless, stainless––the blood that ran through the veins of Jesus was the blood of Jehovah God (Acts 20:28). The blood is the price Jesus paid for our redemption.

The result of the giving of the blood is "the forgiveness of sins." In the Old Testament God thundered out (and He has not changed His mind), "The soul that sinneth, it shall die!" Again, through the prophet, God said, "All we like sheep have gone astray." Through the New Testament writer, the Holy Ghost declares, "All have sinned and come short of the glory of God." Through the beloved John, the Holy Spirit has given to us the definition of sin: "Whosoever committeth sin TRANS-GRESSETH ALSO THE LAW: FOR SIN IS THE TRANS-

GRESSION OF THE LAW" (I John 3:4). Therefore, according to the standard of Jehovah God we are all supposed to be in hell; but God in His grace provided a way of escape. However, "without shedding of blood is no remission" (Heb. 9:22). "The blood of Jesus Christ, God's Son, cleanseth us . . ." (I John 1:7). In the book of Leviticus, ten times the Holy Spirit connects the atonement of the blood with the forgiveness of the sinner's sins. Jehovah God knows no other way except the bloodway. It has been God's way since the Garden of Eden. Adam was covered with the skins produced by a blood sacrifice . . . innocent animals gave their blood to provide coats of skins for Adam and Eve. Later, the son of Adam thought he would get away with a bloodless offering——but he did not. Abel "by faith" brought a blood offering and God accepted it. Cain, in his own wisdom, brought fruit . . . bloodless. God rejected Cain's offering. Since that hour God has demanded blood——and without blood there is no remission! By every animal, innocent and without blemish, slain in sacrifice according to the direction of Jehovah God, God was saying through the death of that animal, "MY Lamb, My Son, is going to die!"

Then one day, John the Baptist pointed to a Man and cried out, "Behold the Lamb of God that taketh away the sin of the world!" (John 1:29).

A little later, on a cruel cross planted on Mount Calvary, the Lamb of God poured out His blood. The eternal purpose of Jehovah God was achieved. Jesus said before He died, "IT IS FINISHED!" (John 19:30). What a marvelous statement——in our language only three words, but in those three words He was saying, "I have accomplished what I came to accomplish! My Father's plan for remission of sins is complete. My blood has been shed. I have laid my life down. It is accomplished!"

Men of God who have studied the language and the

customs of the day of Jesus tell us that the word "redeem" has to do with slaves . . . men and women who were bought and sold in the slave market. Of course, we (all of us) were slaves to sin, in bondage to the master of sin, the devil; but now those of us who have received Jesus are free-born sons of God. We belong to the family of God, the household of God; and since we are the sons of God in Christ Jesus, bone of His bone, flesh of His flesh, we who are born again ". . . have the mind of Christ" (I Cor. 2:16). Therefore, Jesus is able to take us into His intimate confidence and make known to us who are born again believers, the mystery hidden in the ages behind us. Jesus says to all true, born again children of God, "Henceforth (from this day on) I call you not servants; for the servant knoweth not what his lord doeth: but I have called you friends; for all things that I have heard of my Father I have made known unto you" (John 15:15). What a glorious revelation!

Through the blood we have forgiveness of sins; and the forgiveness of our sins is "ACCORDING TO THE RICHES OF HIS GRACE." I am sure you who are saved will agree with me that there are not enough adjectives in all the languages of all the world to describe the riches of God's grace. Thank God, I am forgiven through the riches of His grace . . . not the meager labor of my hands!

Verses 8–12: "Wherein He hath abounded toward us in all wisdom and prudence; having made known unto us the mystery of His will, according to His good pleasure which He hath purposed in Himself: that in the dispensation of the fulness of times He might gather together in one all things in Christ, both which are in Heaven, and which are on earth; even in Him: In whom also we have obtained an inheritance, being predestinated according to the purpose of Him who worketh all things after the counsel of His own will: That we should be to the praise of His glory, who first trusted in Christ."

Certainly we will never understand all Scripture. There is much of it past finding out so far as the finite creature is concerned; but it is the good pleasure of Jesus to reveal unto the spiritually minded the deep things of the Scriptures. For instance: ". . . Eye hath not seen, nor ear heard, neither have entered into the heart of man, the things which God hath prepared for them that love Him. BUT GOD hath revealed them unto us by His Spirit: for the Spirit searcheth all things, yea, the deep things of God" (I Cor. 2:9–10).

Again: "But ye have an unction from the Holy One, and ye know all things . . . But the anointing which ye have received of Him abideth in you, and ye need not that any man teach you: but as the same anointing teacheth you of all things, and is truth, and is no lie, and even as He hath taught you, ye shall abide in Him" (I John 2:20 and 27).

It is the good pleasure of God to reveal unto us the deep things of the Word, and of the world to come. He has abounded toward us in all wisdom and prudence. James invites: "If any man lack wisdom, let him ask of God." The wise man, Solomon, declared: "The fear of the Lord is the beginning of knowledge."

Paul says, "Having made known unto us the mystery of His will, according to His good pleasure which He hath purposed in Himself: That in the dispensation of the fulness of times He might gather together in one all things in Christ, both which are in heaven, and which are on earth; even in Him."

The dispensation of the fulness of times is the seventh and last of the dispensational ages. It will be the time when King Jesus will sit on the throne in Jerusalem and reign over the house of Israel in the Millennial Kingdom here on this earth. You will find the description of this kingdom in II Samuel 7:8–17, Zech. 12:8, Isaiah 11.

In Luke 1:31–33 the Holy Spirit tells the virgin Mary that her son will be called Jesus, He will be great, He will be the Son of God——and that He will sit on the throne of His father David.

Some dear Christians feed only on the milk of the Word. Of course, the milk is good——but we need to go on to strong meat. The redemption purchased by the blood of Jesus Christ does not stop with the redemption of the soul. All creation will be delivered from the curse, all creation will be set free in the fulness of times. For instance, Paul sets forth the glorious truth that there is no condemnation to them which are in Christ Jesus, and that the sufferings of this present time are not worthy to be compared with the glory which shall be revealed in us. He goes on to say, "For the earnest expectation of the creature waiteth for the manifestation of the sons of God (that will be at the Rapture of the church). For the creature was made subject to vanity, not willingly, but by reason of Him who hath subjected the same in hope (referring to Jesus Christ and the redemption He purchased through His blood). Because the creature itself also shall be delivered from the bondage of corruption into the glorious liberty of the children of God. (The *creature* refers to all creation——earth, the animal kingdom and the solar system. All things will be made new.) FOR WE KNOW THAT THE WHOLE CREATION GROANETH AND TRAVAILETH IN PAIN TOGETHER UNTIL NOW. And not only they, *but ourselves also*, which have the first fruits of the Spirit, even we ourselves GROAN WITHIN OURSELVES waiting for the adoption, to wit, THE REDEMPTION OF OUR BODY" (Rom. 8:19–23).

Paul said, "ourselves also." That refers to himself, and to every believer. Beloved, as long as we remain on this earth we are not at home. We are strangers, we are among enemies. As long as we remain in this body we will groan and suffer. Even those of us who have the first fruits of the Spirit groan and travail. We are looking forward to the blessed hope and the glorious appearing of Jesus, when we will receive our glorified bodies.

Please notice *the redemption of the body*. With His blood Jesus purchased redemption, deliverance, freedom ––for all of God's creation. Please do not think that I am suggesting that animals can be born again. That is not so. But if you will read Isaiah 11 you will discover that the Kingdom on earth will have an abundance of animals: The bear, the lamb, the kid, the lion, the snake, and there will be no killing, no destroying in God's holy mountain, the Kingdom. This earth will be delivered from the bondage of corruption, and there will be peace on earth when the knowledge of the Lord covers the earth as the waters now cover the sea.

THE BEST IS YET TO COME! In verse 11 we read, "In whom (Jesus) also we have obtained an inheritance, being predestinated according to the purpose of Him who worketh all things after the counsel of His own will." Jesus is the provider of all spiritual blessings. The Greek word for "inheritance" suggests that we have an allotment. In other words, in Jesus we are allotted an eternal inheritance. Paul is speaking here of us who were outcasts, aliens from the commonwealth of Israel, stripped of all the promises and the covenants, deserving nothing, without God and without hope. We *in Christ* are "heirs of God, and joint-heirs with Christ" (Rom. 8:17). In Jesus, "All things are yours" (I Cor. 3:21–23). What a boundless inheritance! Certainly far past all human understanding. The person who is born again has at his disposal all that heaven affords.

"We have obtained an inheritance." But in the Lord Jesus Christ "We were made a heritage." That is, the Lord Jesus will inherit us. We who are believers make up the New Testament church (I Cor. 12:12–13, Eph. 5:27). Jesus will present to Himself the church without spot or wrinkle; therefore, we are His heritage . . . His inheritance. At the marriage supper in the sky, the Bride (the New Testament church made up of all born again, blood washed, redeemed children of God) will be presented to the Lord Jesus . . . His inheritance . . . in that day when He makes up His jewels. It was for this joy set before the Lord Jesus that He endured the cross . . . He did not *enjoy* the cross, He *endured* it, despising the shame; but for the joy on the other side of the cross, namely, the church without spot or wrinkle, He set His eye upon Calvary and marched on to the horrible agony, the shedding of His blood for the remission of sin——the redemption price of the sinner. Through His blood, He purchased sinners for His very own.

THEREFORE: "Beloved, now are we the sons of God, and it doth not yet appear what we shall be: but we know that, when He shall appear, we shall be like Him; for we shall see Him as He is. And every man that hath this hope in him purifieth himself, even as He is pure" (I John 3:2–3).

"Beloved" . . . what a wonderful position, what a wonderful condition! In Jesus, redeemed, adopted, sons of the living God, members of the body of Christ, seated in the heavenlies with Jesus. The most glorious of the glory is the fact that we are NOW the possessors of these tremendous spiritual blessings.

Let us now go on to . . .

THE HOLY SPIRIT'S PART IN OUR REDEMPTION

God the Father so loved sinners that He gave His only begotten Son. God the Son so loved sinners that He left the bosom of the Father, came to earth's sorrow, and willingly laid down His life that we hell-deserving sinners might have life. But there is a Third Person who has a very definite part in our redemption:

Verses 13 and 14: "In whom ye also trusted, after that ye heard the word of truth, the gospel of your salvation: in whom also after that ye believed, ye were sealed with that Holy Spirit of promise, which is the earnest of our inheritance until the redemption of the purchased possession, unto the praise of His glory."

There could be no salvation apart from the Holy Spirit. I am so thankful that God loved us, I am so thankful that Jesus died for us——but I am also thankful that He, the Holy Ghost, came into the world, to "reprove the world of sin, and of righteousness, and of judgment: Of sin, because they believe not on me; of righteousness, because I go to my Father, and ye see me no more; of judgment, because the prince of this world is judged" (John 16:9—11).

Jesus instructed the disciples that it was imperative that He go away, and that if He did not return to heaven the Spirit would not come; but if He departed He would send the Comforter; and when the Comforter (which is the Holy Ghost) was come, He would reprove the world of sin, of righteousness and of judgment. The Holy Ghost, the Third Person of the Trinity, convicts us of sin; and certainly there could be no conversion minus Holy Spirit conviction.

The third chapter of John's Gospel gives us the interview between Jesus and Nicodemus. Nicodemus was an outstanding religionist, but he had a hungry heart. He sought out Jesus, and began his conversation by saying:

"We know that thou art a teacher come from God: for no man can do these miracles that thou doest, except God be with Him. Jesus answered and said unto him, . . . Except a man be born again, he cannot see the kingdom of God." Nicodemus asked, "How can a man be born when he is old?" Jesus answered, "Except a man be born of water and of the Spirit, he cannot enter into the kingdom of God."

The *water* is the Word (John 4:10, 14, 26 and 27; John 15:3; Eph. 5:26; I Peter 1:23). The water is the *Word*—it is not the river Jordan nor a lovely baptistry in your church building. The Spirit in John 3:5 is, of course, the Holy Spirit. Let me point out the part the Holy Spirit has in our redemption:

God the Father planned our salvation in the eternity behind us.

God the Son provided and purchased our salvation in the fulness of time.

The Spirit of God *applied* our salvation. The Holy Ghost persuaded us to accept salvation. "The natural man receiveth not the things of God." No person could ever believe or receive the Word of God apart from the power of the Holy Spirit.

Jesus said concerning the Spirit, "When He does come, He shall not speak of Himself. HE SHALL TAKE OF MINE AND SHOW IT UNTO YOU!" (John 16:13–15). The Holy Ghost is in the world during this Dispensation of Grace, to point men to the Lamb of God. He is not in the world to magnify Himself; He is in the world to make known the gift of God: *Salvation through the shed blood of the Lord Jesus Christ.*

In John 6:44 we find, "No man can come to me, except the Father which hath sent me draw him." Sinners are drawn to God through the power of the Holy Spirit (John 16:7-9). When the sinner hears the Word of God, the Holy Spirit through and by the Word of God opens the eyes of understanding. "If our Gospel be hid, it is hid to them that are lost: In whom the god of this world hath blinded the minds of them which believe not, lest the light of the glorious Gospel of Christ, who is the image of God, should shine unto them" (II Cor. 4:3-4). The Spirit opens the eyes of the mind, the understanding of the heart, and makes known to us the glorious fact that Jesus finished salvation, and that it is only through faith that we can become the possessor of the gift of God. This is the initial work of the Holy Ghost in our salvation.

In Romans 10 Paul gives us a clear outline of salvation: "For whosoever shall call upon the name of the Lord shall be saved. How then shall they call on Him in whom they have not believed? And how shall they believe in Him of whom they have not heard? and how shall they hear without a preacher? And how shall they preach, except they be sent?" (Rom. 10:13ff).

God calls preachers.

God's preachers preach the Gospel.

The Gospel is the light. Jesus said, "I am the light of the world." In Psalm 119:105 we read, "Thy Word is a lamp . . . ." Psalm 119:130 tells us, "The entrance of thy Words giveth light."

The Holy Ghost, through the Word, opens the darkened intelligence——the mind that is blinded by the devil; and when the poor sinner sees his lost condition and in the same instant sees the sacrifice Jesus made to save

51

sinners, through the enlightening power of the Holy Ghost that sinner is drawn to the gift of God. The Holy Ghost draws sinners to Jesus—then, seeing the glorious gift of God, the sinner desires the gift of God. Therefore, the Holy Ghost sees to it that faith enters the heart, and the sinner calls, "Lord, remember me," or "God, be merciful to me, a sinner," or "Lord Jesus, I receive you now as my Saviour." The words are not what counts— it is what happens in the heart that is important.

When we receive from the heart the Word of God, the Word is the seed that brings the new birth. But the Word will never enter the heart until the heart is made ready by the enlightening power of the Holy Ghost.

The Holy Ghost first draws us to Jesus (John 6:44).

The Holy Ghost then "borns" us into the family of God (John 3:5).

We are baptized into the body of Christ by the Holy Ghost (I Cor. 12:13).

The Holy Ghost takes up His abode in our heart (Rom. 8:9).

The Holy Spirit leads us (Rom. 8:14).

The Holy Spirit assures us (Rom. 8:16).

The Holy Spirit seals us until the day of redemption (Eph. 4:30, Eph. 1:14).

The Holy Spirit has a future part in the completion of our redemption. We will be quickened by the Spirit when the Rapture occurs (Rom. 8:11). Jesus is the Lord of the quick (the living) and the dead, and through the power of the Spirit the bodies of the saints who have died will be raised, and the bodies of the saints who are living when the Rapture occurs will be changed in a moment . . . "in the twinkling of an eye."

There is no such thing as salvation apart from the

Spirit of God. A person who does not possess the Holy Spirit is not a child of God. There is much ignorance—yea, gross ignorance—concerning the ministry of the Spirit in this Dispensation of Grace. All born again persons possess the Holy Spirit. It is true that not all born again persons are *filled* with the Holy Spirit, as we will learn later in this Epistle; but there is no spiritual birth apart from the Holy Spirit of God. Birth by the Holy Spirit is the only entrance into the kingdom of God. Anything short of the spiritual birth through the power of the Holy Ghost in connection with the precious Word of God is not salvation. All that God the Father has done, all that God the Father has sacrificed, all that Jesus has done, all of the agony and suffering through which He passed, cannot save—*apart from* the gracious work of the Holy Spirit.

Let me sum it up in these words:

The salvation planned by God the Father and *purposed* for us, the salvation *purchased* for us by the Son of God through His blood, is made over to us personally, and becomes our *personal possession* by the power of the Spirit.

In closing this section, let me remind you that our redemption was settled in the eternity behind us (I Peter 1:18ff). Redemption purchased by the blood of Jesus Christ continues through the eternity that lies ahead of us. The gracious work of redemption has been provided from eternity through eternity, by the Trinity. In the eternity behind us,

God the Father chose (or elected) us to be His very own . . . the church, the body of Christ, made up of born again believers.

The Son of God purchased us with His own precious

53

blood. Jesus willingly gave His life that we might be saved, and

The Holy Spirit persuaded us (those of us who are saved) to believe the record God has given of His Son. The Holy Spirit enlightened our blinded minds, opened our hard hearts, and worked the miracle of the new birth through the seed of the Word (I Peter 1:23).

For those of us who are born again, this is in the past. What does redemption present to us today? God the Father has given to us the position of sons NOW. We are born sons of God, we are the adopted sons of God, we enjoy every privilege of an adult son. The Lord Jesus Christ reveals to us His intimate mind and will. We have the mind of Christ through the indwelling Spirit. The Holy Spirit NOW seals us and guarantees to us that we are God's very own. We are sealed with the Holy Spirit of promise——NOW!

But what about redemption in the future? God the Father will receive us and accept us because of the price paid in the blood of His only begotten Son. He will say to us in the future, "Enter thou the joys of thy Lord." The Son of God, the Lord Jesus, will inherit us in the body——the Church——when we are presented to Him without spot or wrinkle or any such thing (Eph. 5:26) and we will be displayed in the heavenlies to show the exceeding riches of God's grace (Eph. 2:6–7). In the future the Spirit will claim us, along with the Father and the Son, because He (the Holy Spirit) is co-equal with the Father and the Son in our redemption.

PAUL PRAYS FOR THE BELIEVER,
THAT HE WILL HAVE KNOWLEDGE AND POWER

Verses 15–18: "Wherefore I also, after I heard of your faith in the Lord Jesus, and love unto all the saints, cease not to give thanks for you, making mention of you in my prayers; that the God of our Lord Jesus Christ, the Father of glory, may give unto you the spirit of wisdom and revelation in the knowledge of Him: The eyes of your understanding being enlightened; that ye may know what is the hope of His calling, and what the riches of the glory of His inheritance in the saints."

You will notice that in all of Paul's letters to the different churches, he reminds them that he faithfully prays for them; but in this particular letter he does more than that. He enumerates the requests which he makes known to God in their behalf: That they might have wisdon and revelation in the knowledge of Jesus, that their eyes of understanding might be enlightened, that they might know "what is the hope of His calling, the riches of the glory of His inheritance in the saints."

Paul could not pray such a prayer as this in behalf of the *Corinthians*, because most of them were still living on milk . . . they were not strong enough Christians to receive the meat of the Word. Paul prays here for a spiritually minded group in Ephesus.

Notice verse 15 begins with the word "wherefore," thus connecting the prayer with what preceded it. In his petition, Paul is praying that God will reveal to the individual believers in Ephesus not only the doctrine concerning their redemption (that is, that God the Father, God the Son, and God the Holy Spirit all had a part in redeeming them), but that they will also come into a personal knowledge and a personal experience, knowing the source and the secret of the power to live and walk daily as a believer should, since we are members of the body of Christ.

In verse 16, Paul reminds these believers that he gives thanks for them in his prayers. He was thankful for a group such as the one in the church at Ephesus.

In verse 17 we find the key to Christian knowledge: "REVELATION." In all of his letters Paul is very careful to make plain the fact that his message came by revelation——not by man, not through man, but from God by direct revelation. The Word of God consists, for the most part, of knowledge which man cannot know nor receive except by revelation. If we understand the things of the past, if we look into the future, we must rely upon God to unveil deep spiritual truths to us as we yield to the Holy Spirit, the Teacher of the Word of God (I John 2:27). The Holy Spirit gives to us wisdom, knowledge and understanding——but only through revelation.

One phase of the ministry of the Holy Spirit in this Dispensation of Grace is to reveal the deep things of God to spiritually minded believers. Study carefully John 16:12–15. There are many Christians who read the Bible ——but there are few Christians who *study* the Bible. Almost anyone can read a chapter a day, and from that chapter learn things about Jesus, God, heaven, hell . . . but to dig into the diamond mines and the gold mines, to find the unsearchable riches of the Word of God, we must be led by the Holy Ghost, enlightened by the Holy Ghost ——and if we ever understand the deep things of God it must be through the revelation of the Holy Ghost as we study.

In verse 18 we learn of the channel of Christian knowledge: AN ENLIGHTENED HEART. In the King James version we have, "The eyes of your understanding being enlightened," but in the original language it is "the eyes of your heart" (the inner man)——not the natural eyes or mind, but the spiritual eyes. The eyes of the heart, of the inner man, are the organs of light, spiritually speaking. Until the Holy Spirit has wrought His regenerating work in us, the eyes of the heart are blinded. The person who has never been born again cannot know the things of God: "But the natural man receiveth not the things of the Spirit of God: for they are foolishness unto him: neither can he know them, because they are spiritually discerned" (I Cor. 2:14). But when the eyes of the inner man are opened through the power of the Holy Spirit, we grow in knowledge and understanding of spiritual truths. There are many born again people who need to pray daily, and daily yield themselves to the Holy Spirit, allowing the Spirit to open their eyes that they may see the great truths God has laid down in His Word concerning our present possession in Christ, and the things that lie ahead for those of us who are born again believers.

Please notice the last part of verse 18 and the first part of verse 19––and you will see that Paul is not praying for spiritual insight and knowledge in order that the Ephesians might boast or brag about their spirituality; but he wants them to appreciate the blessings and the benefits they enjoy because of their redemption. The average believer is totally ignorant and unappreciative concerning his present spiritual possession.

Beloved, if you are born again, you are *somebody*, whether you have realized it or not! You are now a son of God. You now possess the divine nature of God. In your bosom dwells the Holy Spirit. You are led by the Holy Spirit. Your citizenship is in heaven. *In Jesus you are somebody*. To the spiritually minded believer, this does not puff one up, nor cause one to be proud. On the contrary, the more we learn about our spiritual possessions and privileges, the more humble we should become. If you listen to people testify in a public meeting, you can always measure their spirituality by the testimony they give. Yes, sad but so, most Christians are totally ignorant concerning our position and our possession in the Lord Jesus.

Paul prays that they will understand "the hope of His calling, and . . . the riches of the glory of His inheritance in the saints." Paul wants all believers to comprehend the unspeakable preciousness and power of our redemption; the inheritance held in store for us; also the glory of it——and the riches of its glory.

It is the joy and the good pleasure of God to bless His children. At His right hand there are pleasures forevermore, and no good thing will He withhold from them that walk uprightly. If we seek first the Kingdom of God and His righteousness, all these other things will be added unto us. If we can only realize the riches we possess now, we will not be such spiritual paupers, and we will appreciate much more the inheritance that lies ahead.

Verse 19: "And what is the exceeding greatness of His power to us-ward who believe, according to the working of His mighty power."

In this verse, Paul wants us to understand "what is the exceeding greatness of His power" toward us who believe. Every born again child of God has within his bosom the power of Almighty God. We are *kept* by the power of God. Jesus does not redeem a soul——and then leave that soul alone to fight the warfare of faith. Promises such as these encourage Christians to move on in the spiritual life:

"I will never leave thee nor forsake thee . . . that we may boldly say, God is my helper."

"I can do all things through Christ which strengtheneth me."

"We know that all things work together for good to

58

them that love God, to them who are the called according to His purpose."

"There hath no temptation taken you but such as is common to man; but God is faithful, who will not suffer (allow) you to be tempted above that ye are able, but will with the temptation make a way to escape, that ye may be able to bear it."

"If any man lack wisdom, let him ask of God."

"Who shall separate us from the love of Christ? Shall tribulation, or distress, or persecution, or famine, or nakedness, or peril, or sword? As it is written, For thy sake we are killed all the day long; we are accounted as sheep for the slaughter. NAY, in all these things we are more than conquerors through Him that loved us. For I am persuaded, that neither death, nor life, nor angels, nor principalities, nor powers, nor things present, nor things to come, nor height, nor depth, nor any other creature, SHALL BE ABLE TO SEPARATE US FROM THE LOVE OF GOD, WHICH IS IN CHRIST JESUS OUR LORD!" (Rom. 8:35–39).

"WHAT SHALL WE THEN SAY TO THESE THINGS? IF GOD BE FOR US, WHO CAN BE AGAINST US?" (Rom. 8:31).

When the believer discovers these promises and thousands of others just as precious, he will march on to victory in Christ Jesus, through the power of God. God's power is not only great––HIS POWER IS "EXCEEDING GREAT" . . . *the exceeding greatness of His power.* As we go into the next verse you will note that this exceeding great power comes through the Lord Jesus Christ.

Verses 20–23: "Which He wrought in Christ when He raised Him from the dead, and set Him at His own right hand in the heavenly places, far above all principality, and power, and might, and dominion, and every name that is named, not only in this world, but also in that which is to come: And hath put all things under His feet, and gave Him to be the head over all things to the church, which is His body, the fulness of Him that filleth all in all."

In these verses we have the guarantee of these blessings to all believers, because they are wrought *in Christ*. All spiritual blessings are "according to the working of His mighty power, which He wrought in Christ." The literal Greek reads, "the manifested strength of His indwelling might." This "indwelling might" possessed by the Lord Jesus Christ was manifested in two ways:

(1) *Through His resurrection from the dead.* Jesus promised His followers He would rise from the dead the third day, and that is exactly what He did. That is the one outstanding fact that sets Him apart from and above all other great men in the religious realm. There have been men who founded great religions––and please notice I said *"religions."* For example, Confucius, Buddha, Mary Baker Eddy, Joseph Smith, Pastor Russell and others became head of great religious movements. They are dead and gone, and no one has seen them since. The resurrection of Jesus Christ proves that He is very God.

(2) *Through His exaltation to His present position at the right hand of God the Father.* How on this earth could anyone suggest that God's program of redemption could fail, with such power placed at our disposal? We have within our bosom the power of Almighty God, and if we as believers stagger and stumble and fall, it is our fault––not God's. God has not only provided redemption for the sinner, but also complete and total victory for the believer!

We learn in verses 21 and 22 that Christ has been

exalted to a position of absolute, universal authority. He has been made *"the head over all things to the church which is His body."* This power, the exceeding great power, possessed by Jesus Christ is administered through His exalted person, and is administered from His exalted position in heaven. He (the Exalted One) is the head of the church which is His body. We are members of His body, bone of His bone, flesh of His flesh (Eph. 5:30). Therefore this exceeding great power is transmitted to us (the body) from the head (the Lord Jesus).

God is looking for believers who will commit themselves unto Him, and allow Him to enlighten their hearts so that they can see and know the spiritual power and privileges they enjoy in the redemption that is in Christ Jesus. God in regeneration becomes the author of faith in our heart, which faith makes us sons of God. God is the author of inner life, the new life, the new creation which dwells in the bosom of every believer; but He does not stop there: Because of our redemption He becomes the controller of the motives and intents of the heart—— (providing the believer will yield his heart into the hands of God). God inspires the heart, and makes provision spiritually and physically for the believer if the believer will only surrender fully and allow God to enlighten and direct him day by day.

"That if thou shalt confess with thy mouth the Lord Jesus, and shalt believe in thine heart that God hath raised Him from the dead, thou shalt be saved. For with the heart man believeth unto righteousness; and with the mouth confession is made unto salvation" (Rom. 10:9–10). Wicked hands nailed Jesus to the cross. He was wounded for our transgressions, He was bruised for our iniquities. All we like sheep have gone astray, but Jehovah laid on Jesus the iniquity of us all. Yes, Jesus was smitten of God and afflicted, that we might be saved. He was nailed to a cross, He died, they buried Him; but God raised Him up from the dead and exalted Him at God's own right hand in the heavenlies. God has exalted Jesus *far above* all principality and power, might and dominion, above every name that is named——not only in this world, but also in that which is to come. God has exalted His Son far above any and all, in heaven or in earth——or in the world to come! God has put all things under the feet of Jesus. God gave Him the position as head over all things to the church, "which is the body of Christ, the fulness of Him that filleth all in all." Jesus purchased the church at the tremendous price of Calvary (read Acts 20:28). Jesus is the head of the True Church (Eph. 5:23). We are members connected to the head (Eph. 5:30). He is also the foundation of the New Testament church (I Cor. 3:11). He is the author and the finisher of our faith (Heb. 12:1–2). We who are saved do not belong to an organization; we are connected to an *organism*——the Lord Jesus Christ.

1. And you hath he quickened, who were dead in trespasses and sins:

2. Wherein in time past ye walked according to the course of this world, according to the prince of the power of the air, the spirit that now worketh in the children of disobedience:

3. Among whom also we all had our conversation in times past in the lusts of our flesh, fulfilling the desires of the flesh and of the mind; and were by nature the children of wrath, even as others.

4. But God, who is rich in mercy, for his great love wherewith he loved us,

5. Even when we were dead in sins, hath quickened us together with Christ, (by grace ye are saved;)

6. And hath raised us up together, and made us sit together in heavenly places in Christ Jesus:

7. That in the ages to come he might shew the exceeding riches of his grace in his kindness toward us through Christ Jesus.

8. For by grace are ye saved through faith; and that not of yourselves: it is the gift of God:

9. Not of works, lest any man should boast.

10. For we are his workmanship, created in Christ Jesus unto good works, which God hath before ordained that we should walk in them.

11. Wherefore remember, that ye being in time past Gentiles in the flesh, who are called Uncircumcision by that which is called the Circumcision in the flesh made by hands;

12. That at that time ye were without Christ, being aliens from the commonwealth of Israel, and strangers from the covenants of promise, having no hope, and without God in the world:

13. But now in Christ Jesus ye who sometimes were far off are made nigh by the blood of Christ.

14. For he is our peace, who hath made both one, and hath broken down the middle wall of partition between us;

15. Having abolished in his flesh the enmity, even the law of commandments contained in ordinances; for to make in himself of twain one new man, so making peace;

16. And that he might reconcile both unto God in one body by the cross, having slain the enmity thereby:

17. And came and preached peace to you which were afar off, and to them that were nigh.

18. For through him we both have access by one Spirit unto the Father.

19. Now therefore ye are no more strangers and foreigners, but fellowcitizens with the saints, and of the household of God;

20. And are built upon the foundation of the apostles and prophets, Jesus Christ himself being the chief corner stone;

21. In whom all the building fitly framed together groweth unto an holy temple in the Lord:

22. In whom ye also are builded together for an habitation of God through the Spirit.

THE METHOD OF GENTILE SALVATION

In this chapter we will see the most wonderful body ever formed. Speaking to the believers at Ephesus, Paul begins chapter two by saying,

Verse 1: "And you hath He quickened, who were dead in trespasses and sins." The word "quickened" means "to make alive." To these Gentiles at Ephesus Paul is saying, "You have been made alive, you have been resurrected from the dead."

In the beginning, God created the heaven and the earth. In the process of time, He brought order out of chaos. The Spirit of God moved upon the face of the waters, and God began to create anew. I believe this happened six thousand years ago. After God had separated the water from the land, and brought the sun, moon, and stars into view, when all the animals had been created and vegetation had appeared . . . when everything was "good," God climaxed His creative work by saying, "LET US MAKE MAN."

There are varied and sundry teachings concerning man . . . how he came to be, from what he came, how long it has taken man to reach the place where he is today. But unless you are an atheist or an evolutionist, the answer is in Genesis 1:26: "And God said, LET US MAKE MAN IN OUR IMAGE, AFTER OUR LIKENESS." God created man, and man was God's own.

God planted a magnificent garden and placed Adam in that garden. The first assignment God gave to Adam was the naming of all the animals . . . and whatever Adam called them, that is the name God gave them. Everything went fine for awhile——and then God saw the loneliness of man. Knowing it was not good for man to be alone, God created and presented His first gift to man:

It must have been very calm and quiet in the Garden of Eden. God put Adam to sleep, and the Great Surgeon performed His first operation. No doubt all creation waited ——wondering, expecting. The trees of the garden provided the shade for God's hospital. The Holy Spirit arranged every detail according to God's divine instruction. Adam was asleep——the incision was made, a rib was removed. God closed the incision and "the rib, which the Lord God had taken from man, made He a woman, and brought her unto the man."

There is no doubt in my mind that Eve was indescribably lovely, and very charming. She was dignified; she was the queen of all creation. She was as refreshing as the morning dew in May. She was clothed with a snow-white garment down to her feet . . . Shekinah glory (God's holiness) danced about her body. Perhaps Adam could not believe his own eyes as he looked upon the marvelous helpmate God had brought unto him. (God is a *good* God ——but remember, beloved, He is also *"a consuming fire"* ——Heb. 12:29.)

It is the good pleasure of God to bless His children ——and Adam was His child by creation. God gave Eve to Adam. Eve was the first sweetheart of this earth. In Adam's case, it was love at first sight. The wedding took place in God's great open-air cathedral. God, who was the father of the bride, gave her away. The royal surgeon stood at the groom's side. The Holy Spirit performed the ceremony and pronounced Adam and Eve man and wife——one flesh. Surely the angels must have sung a song! Adam and Eve did not go anywhere on their honeymoon. They were in the most beautiful spot on this earth——the Garden of Eden. The two lovers, God's first man and woman, walked away hand in hand, and the angels must have smiled.

Time passed. How long Adam and Eve lived in the Garden in the peace and quiet of its beauty, I do not know; but tragedy struck. They sinned . . . and by sinning they forfeited their joyous companionship with God. Many things have changed in this old world . . . we have the radio, the telephone, color television, space rockets, electronic brains . . . but some things are unaltered. *Man in his need for God is the same.* Poor Adam! When he sinned, he saw that he was naked——and every unregenerated man today is just as Adam was . . . naked before God!

Remember——the devil suggested to Eve that the reason God did not want her to eat of the tree of the knowledge of good and evil was because God knew that the day she ate of the fruit, her eyes would be opened, she would *know*, and she would become "as gods." In other words, she would become a little god.

When Adam and Eve sinned and their eyes were opened, they immediately put their wisdom and knowledge to work. They sewed fig leaves together——and I am sure the garments they made covered the nakedness of their flesh. The green fig leaves, with the frills of the leaves rightly placed, undoubtedly made a very beautiful garment. Poor Adam! He was covered . . . so far as he knew. His spiritual mind had been darkened——blacked out and blinded by sin. God had told Adam that the day he ate of the tree of the knowledge of good and evil he would surely die. He did die *spiritually* that moment——and every man, woman or child born into the world since Adam's fall is dead in trespasses and sin.

Adam thought everything was all right until he heard the voice of God. The smile left his face. He looked at Eve . . . they trembled, and ran to hide.

"They heard the voice of the Lord God walking in the garden in the cool of the day: and Adam and his wife hid themselves from the presence of the Lord God amongst the trees of the garden" (Gen. 3:8).

In the next few moments, Adam learned what many men need to learn today: The labors of man's hands cannot satisfy God! What looks good to man does not necessarily look good to God. Adam learned that his garment was inadequate to hide the guilt of his conscience! In God's eyes, Adam was still naked. He also learned that he could not hide from God. The trees did not separate him from the eyes of his Creator. Man needs to learn today that while there are many religions that look good——man cannot hide from God under these religious cloaks.

Adam learned something else: His excuses did not clear him of his guilt. He put the blame on Eve. Eve passed it on down to the serpent. Nevertheless, God cursed the woman and the man. Adam's excuses did not satisfy God. Adam discovered that the labor of his hands could not cover his shame before the eyes of God; the trees of the garden could not hide him from the presence of God; and the excuses he made were not accepted by God (there *was* no excuse). Certainly the children of Adam have not changed. Tens of thousands of men and women are still manufacturing their own coverings, religiously speaking. Today you can hear the sons and daughters of Adam saying things like this:

"We have such beautiful services at our church, our religion is such a beautiful religion. We have such a dignified preacher and such a dignified program." Beloved, God is not looking for beauty or dignity; He is looking for blood! God condemned the fig-leaf covering, and Himself provided coats of skins. Please notice: *God provided* coats of skins. The innocent animals, at the expense of their life and their blood, furnished the coats. God Himself made the coats, and covered the naked bodies of Adam and Eve. All that Adam did——all that he could do——was yield to God's covering.

Man was created to be the joy of God's heart; and one glorious day that will be completely and fully realized in the new heaven and the new earth. In Adam all die——in Christ are all made alive.

Verses 2 and 3: "Wherein in time past ye walked according to the course of this world, according to the prince of the power of the air(the devil) the spirit that now worketh in the children of disobedience (the spirit of wickedness, lust, and sin): Among whom also we all had our conversation in times past (Note: ALL . . . all we like sheep have gone astray . . . there is none righteous, no, not one) in the lusts of our flesh, fulfilling the desires of the flesh and of the mind; and were by nature (born in a natural body handed down by our first parents Adam and Eve . . . a body naturally depraved and sinful) the children of wrath (the devil) even as others (ALL others)."

What a picture! What a sordid, despicable, ugly picture. Yes, WHAT A PICTURE! Dead, walking according to the course of a world steeped in sin, walking according to the dictates of the devil, following the spirit of disobedience, refusing to obey, always disobeying, having conversation in lust, filth, the gutter of the flesh; practicing what the mind suggests, following the desires of lust and of a mind totally depraved, by nature the children of the devil . . . BUT GOD!

Suppose we return to the Garden of Eden for just a moment. God had created only one son and one daughter.

God gave that son everything that man has fought and died to gain——but has never gained! Adam was the dictator of the whole universe. He was in charge of the known earth at that time. He had dominion over everything. And then——God gave him a perfect wife. God requested of him only one thing: "Do not eat of the tree of the knowledge of good and evil."

When Adam deliberately disobeyed God and did exactly what God told him not to do, could not God have annihilated Adam and Eve, and kept a clear conscience in so doing? Could not God have turned the Garden of Eden over to angels and cherubims? Yes, He could have ——but He did not. God in His love and mercy provided a covering . . . and in Genesis 3:15 He promised Jesus, His only begotten Son, who would eventually crush the head of the devil, bring order out of chaos, and give to man a new heaven and a new earth "wherein dwelleth righteousness" . . . BUT GOD!

In verses one through three in our present chapter, Paul paints the picture of a sinner; but in spite of our wretchedness, God loved us:

Verses 4–10: "BUT GOD, who is RICH IN MERCY, for His GREAT LOVE wherewith He loved us, even when we were dead in sins, hath quickened us together with Christ, (by grace ye are saved;) And hath raised us up together, and made us sit together in heavenly places in Christ Jesus: That in the ages to come He might shew the exceeding riches of His grace in His kindness toward us through Christ Jesus. *For by grace are ye saved through faith; and that not of yourselves: it is the gift of God: not of works, lest any man should boast.* For we are His workmanship, created in Christ Jesus unto good works, which God hath before ordained that we should walk in them."

In chapter two is revealed the truth that by the grace of God––(not by works of righteousness which we have done)––we are His workmanship, CREATED IN CHRIST JESUS. The truth revealed in chapter one (that Christ is exalted to the position of head over all things to the church which is His body) is unfolded for us in chapter two. The work of God the Father, God the Son, and God the Spirit continues. As we saw the Trinity working *as one* in our redemption, just so will we see the continuation of the one-ness of the Trinity in the plan of God for the believer.

In chapter one, we saw that the emphasis was placed upon the Father. The Father holds the prominent place in planning redemption for the soul. And of course, "known unto God are all His works from the beginning." It was God who thought; it was God who provided; it was God who loved; it was God who gave. God sent forth His Son, God commended His love toward us, God gave Jesus to die for us while we were yet sinners. The Lamb was smitten by God, for our transgressions.

In chapter two the emphasis is upon the Son––the Lord Jesus. At Calvary, God's best was on display for man's worst. And through Calvary, God provided grace which brings salvation (Titus 2:11). The center and heart of the message of chapter two is the grace God provided through the blood of Jesus Christ. Grace IS Jesus . . . "we beheld His glory . . . FULL OF GRACE AND TRUTH" (John 1:14).

In the first three verses of chapter two, we see the sordid picture of man as a result of sin. In verse four, God who is rich in mercy, in His great love quickened us (raised us) from the dead with Christ, and has made us to sit together with Christ in heavenly places for the singular purpose of displaying the exceeding riches of

God's grace in the ages that lie ahead. There is no better verse in all the Word of God than verse eight to show the way of salvation. We are saved by God's grace, through faith. Salvation is the gift of God——not of ourselves.

It is very, very important that we keep clearly in mind the connection between chapter one and chapter two of our present study. The key to the connection is the one word "DEAD." Jesus our Saviour, Jesus the Grace of God, in order to provide salvation, took a body a little lower than the angels, for the specific purpose of suffering and dying. By the grace of God Jesus tasted death for every man (Heb. 2:9). Jesus Christ, our Lord and Saviour, became one with us in death. The life story of Jesus in the body can be summed up as follows:

Jesus became dead——but death could not hold Him. He was quickened, raised from the dead; then He was exalted to His present position at the right hand of God in the heavenlies. So——Jesus died, rose again, ascended to the heavenlies. Likewise, WE (those of us who are believers) were dead in trespasses and in sins. As the body of Jesus was quickened from the dead, WE have been raised from the dead (spiritually) and the end of our salvation will be the resurrection of the body, when we will have a body just like Jesus' glorious body (I John 3:1–3).

In our resurrection with Jesus (spiritually speaking) we are now made to sit in the heavenlies in Christ Jesus. Carefully compare Eph. 1:20–21 with Eph. 2:1–6. In these first ten verses of chapter two, we learn what we *were*. We learn that the natural man is totally depraved, his ability to reason concerning spiritual things is entirely blacked out, and apart from the power of God to resurrect the spirit, man would be totally and entirely given

71

over to damnation.

If you will carefully study Romans 1:18 through Romans 3:20* you will find the human race described minutely. Man's sinfulness is laid bare. Anyone who can read need not miss the Bible picture of the unregenerated man. Man in the beginning knew God, but refused to glorify Him AS God. Man changed the truth of God into a lie, and worshipped and served the creature instead of God the Creator. Man did not like to retain God in his knowledge. He pushed God out of his thinking and planning. He rebelled against the authority of God. Therefore, God gave man up! Man forsook the glory of God (the root nature of all sin). The fruit that naturally follows is the despicable practices described in Romans 1:18ff.

If you will study Romans 3:21 through Romans 5:21 you will see what God has done for man in Christ Jesus. You will see the matchless grace, the unsearchable riches of grace whereby God passed judgment over on——or placed upon His own Son the judgment that should have been placed upon each of us. God provided redemption through the blood of His only begotten Son. We are delivered from judgment and wrath by faith——not upon any merit on our part, or by works of righteousness which we might do. Through faith, we appropriate the righteousness of God and the life in God *in Christ*.

The sinner is dead in trespasses and sins. The Holy Spirit does not catalog sins, but simply states that unbelievers are dead through trespasses and sins. Through the disobedience of Adam, the father of us all, death moved upon ALL men . . . for all have sinned. Therefore the life-cord is severed. Death is the result. We are dead spiritually, emotionally and mentally so far as the things of God are concerned. "There is none righteous

*Order my 336-page book on Romans—verse by verse. Price $4.00. The price of the book goes entirely to radio expenses.

72

——no, not one!" We are spiritually dead. "There is none that understandeth, there is none that seeketh after God." We have a darkened intelligence . . . we do not understand; we have a deadened emotion, we do not seek after God. "They are all gone out of the way, they are altogether become unprofitable, there is none that doeth good ——no, not one." All men are in the same category. Therefore——since we are dead in trespasses and sins, since God is holy and pure and cannot look on sin, condone sin nor acquit the wicked, it stands to reason that we cannot do the things that please God until we are born again. And though it may seem strange to you, God cannot do for *us* the things that will please us until we are born again. When we are born again we become a new creation (II Cor. 5:17).

The natural man is disobedient to God . . . he is not subject to the will of God, neither indeed can be. That is the reason so many church members cannot live right ——they are up, and then they are down; they are on, and then they are off; they shout during a revival, and then go back to the world when the revival is over. The answer to their problem is that they have never been made new in Christ Jesus.

The unregenerate man is separated from God. He is sold into slavery. The unregenerate man obeys his master——the devil. In obeying the devil, the unregenerate is naturally disobedient to God. Satan has a three-fold system through which he works:

When Jesus was baptized (Matt. 3) the Holy Ghost descended and remained upon Him, and God the Father said, "This is my beloved Son in whom I am well-pleased." Immediately Jesus was led of the Holy Spirit into the wilderness to be tempted of the devil (Matt. 4). After Jesus had fasted forty days and forty nights, the devil appeared——and the battle began! First, the devil said, "If you are the Son of God, change these stones into bread." Jesus was hungry . . . He had been forty days and forty nights without food or drink; but the devil was tempting Him to major on the minor. Jesus did not come into this world to feed the body——He came to save the soul; and if He had turned those stones into bread He would have been kept so busy making bread He would never have had time to heal the sick, raise the dead, cleanse the lepers and save sinners! Jesus of course knew the devil's scheme, and that from the human standpoint Satan attacked first at the weakest point——hunger. You know, beloved, hunger will drive the natural man to beg, borrow, steal and kill to acquire food to ward off starvation. The devil attacked Jesus at the weakest point——*the lust of the flesh*. Jesus said, "Man shall not live by bread alone, but by every word that proceedeth out of the mouth of God."

Satan did not give up. He took Jesus into the Holy City, placed Him on the pinnacle, and said to Him, "It is written (it is recorded in the Psalms) that God will give His angels charge over thee, and in their hands they shall bear thee up . . . Cast yourself down . . . it will not hurt you . . . that is, IF you are the Son of God!" Jesus answered, "Thou shalt not tempt the Lord thy God." There is the temptation through *the pride of life*. If Jesus had jumped from the pinnacle and escaped without injury, He would have been considered an outstanding person . . . He would have performed a very spectacular act.

But Satan did not give up. He took Jesus up into "an exceeding high mountain" and showed Him all the kingdoms of the world, and said, "Look! These are mine to give to whomsoever I will. All these things will I give thee if thou wilt fall down and worship me!" Thus Jesus could by-pass the cross and still become king of the whole earth. But with Jesus there was no short cut. Therefore He said, "Thou shalt worship the Lord thy God, and Him only shalt thou serve." When Jesus said this, Satan departed. You will find the story in Matthew, chapters three and four, and in Luke chapter four. Read and study these accounts carefully.

John the beloved, in I John (the Joy Book) commands: "Love not the world, neither the things that are in the world. If any man love the world, the love of the Father is not in him. FOR ALL THAT IS IN THE WORLD (1) the lust of the flesh, and (2) the lust of the eyes, and (3) the pride of life, is not of the Father, but is of the world. And the world passeth away, and the lust thereof: but he that doeth the will of God abideth for ever" (I John 2:15–17). So the devil works through three avenues. We have pointed out the threefold system of sin's enslavement.

We are given solemn warning concerning this system:

1. The World—we "walked according to the course of this world." The natural man walks in the way of the world because his nature responds to the desires of the world. The world has what the natural man craves.

2. We walked according to the dictates of Satan . . . "according to the dictates of the prince of the power of the air." This statement reveals to us that Satan has his kingdom in the air just above us, and he is the prince of that kingdom. In II Cor. 4:3–4 we are enlightened that Satan is "god of this world." The unregenerate follows the flesh. "We all had our manner of life in times past, in the lusts of our flesh, fulfilling the desires of the flesh and of the mind." Here is a clear picture of the unregenerate . . . controlled by a sin-prompted, a sin-propelled and a sin-responsive nature, thereby yielding to degraded, unrighteous, ungodly lust and filthy desires.

The last part of verse three in our chapter describes the unregenerate as "by nature the children of wrath." We find in Deuteronomy 25:2 the same Hebrew word that is used here in the Greek—and literally translated it would read "SON OF STROKES" . . . or, "WORTHY TO BE BEATEN." The natural man is dead in sins, of his own free will disobedient to a holy God, therefore he deserves to be beaten . . . he is worthy of stripes. But God put the stripes on Jesus, His only begotten Son; and all you need do to burn in hell is to neglect so great salvation!

Because of the spiritual condition of the natural man, the remedy for sin must go much deeper than conduct or character. It must begin by setting right the source of life . . . the heart, from which proceed the *issues of life*.

The first two words in verse four—"BUT GOD"—announce the turning point of the destiny of the unregenerate. Poor lost man could not help himself. Adam tried —but he failed. Cain thought he was doing fine—but God rejected his beautiful fruit-offering. Man before the flood was progressing, building cities, raising cattle, making music, going in business. There were men of renown—giants; but God repented that he had made man, and declared that He would destroy man. He would have destroyed every single solitary soul on this earth—"But Noah found grace in the eyes of the Lord" (Gen. 6:8) and "By faith Noah, being warned of God of things not seen as yet, moved with fear, prepared an ark to the saving of his house; by the which he condemned the world, and became heir of the righteousness which is by faith (Heb. 11:7).

Left to his own ability, his own provision, his own thinking, man cannot repair the damage done by sin. Salvation is not repairing the *old* man; salvation is the creation of a *new* man.

What God did for hell-deserving sinners is the result of what God IS. God is rich in mercy . . . but His riches, His resources, are God HIMSELF. GOD IS LOVE--and it is only because of His great love toward us that God by His grace permitted Jesus to taste death for every one of us. Had it not been for the exceeding riches of God's love and grace, you and I would burn in hell. What God did for us He did because of what He is. God IS love!

Adam and Eve must have been sick at heart when they realized what a horrible thing they had done. They had been dressed in Shekinah glory--but when they ate the forbidden fruit their covering departed and they gazed upon the shame of their nakedness! What a sad, sordid, despicable sight! Man had lost his holy, pure estate with his Creator. Death had moved in. "BUT GOD"--intervened. God turned death into life. God turned despair into hope. And in the fulness of time hope, redemption, salvation, righteousness was born (Gal. 4:4).

THREE GREAT WORDS
DESCRIBE THE MATCHLESS REMEDY
GOD PROVIDED FOR SINNERS

1. *Mercy:* "But God, who is rich in mercy . . . ." God had a perfect right to mete out judgment and wrath upon Adam. Adam had sinned. God has a perfect right to mete out judgment and wrath upon you and me because we have all sinned. If man is to escape the wrath of God (which he deserves), the escape can come only by and through the undeserved mercy, the unmerited favor, of a holy God. That is exactly what God displayed when He promised the coming of Jesus, in Genesis 3:15. In the fulness of time Jesus was born (Gal. 4:4); He died on the rugged cross while God's creatures mocked, sneered and

77

jeered (Matt. 27; Mark 15; John 19).

IN MERCY GOD IS RICH: "The Lord is merciful and gracious, slow to anger, and plenteous in mercy. He will not always chide: neither will He keep His anger for ever. He hath not dealt with us after our sins; nor rewarded us according to our iniquities. For as the heaven is high above the earth, so great is His mercy toward them that fear Him. As far as the east is from the west, so far hath He removed our transgressions from us. Like as a father pitieth his children, so the Lord pitieth them that fear Him. For He knoweth our frame; He remembereth that we are dust. As for man, his days are as grass: as a flower of the field, so he flourisheth. For the wind passeth over it, and it is gone; and the place thereof shall know it no more. *But the mercy of the Lord is from everlasting to everlasting upon them that fear Him*, and His righteousness unto children's children; to such as keep His covenant, and to those that remember His commandments to do them" (Psalm 103:8—18).

I dare not comment on such Scripture. Read it, and re-read it. Chew it, swallow it, digest it, live by it, die by it!

God has no pleasure in the death of the wicked. God's mercy glories and rejoices in pardon for every sinner who will repent and believe on the Lord Jesus Christ.

2. *Love*: "But God . . . for His great love wherewith He loved us . . . ." Love is the one word that describes the nature of God . . . "God is love." It is natural for love to beget love. It is easy to love someone who loves you, to love someone who is always doing kind things for you and saying nice things about you. But God commended His love toward us in that while we were yet sinners . . . totally depraved, despicable, sordid, ungodly, hateful, hating one another . . . Christ died for us.

78

God commended His love toward such as that; God loved us even when we were dead in sins. The fact that our hopeless, unlovely condition failed to cause God to condemn us and damn us, sets forth the truth that His love is far, far beyond human imagination. As we sing, "Could we with ink the ocean fill, and were the skies of parchment made, were every stalk on earth a quill, and every man a scribe by trade," we could never write or describe the love of God. Such love is beyond human imagination. No wonder the Holy Spirit refers to God's love as "GREAT LOVE."

Love consists of two elements:
(a) desire
(b) delight

Desire is the essence of God's love toward us, even when we were yet sinners. It is God's desire to save the sinner. It was God's desire to cover Adam with coats of skins. Adam yielded . . . submitted to God––and God covered him. It is not God's will that any perish, but that all come to repentance. "Whosoever will, let him drink of the water of life freely." "Whosoever shall call upon the name of the Lord shall be saved." "Him that cometh unto Me I will in no wise cast out." God desires to save every sinner.

His *delight* is in the sinner made a saint––by grace through faith in Jesus, the Son. I think most of us can comprehend the delight of God in a saint. I believe it is easy to see how God could delight in an honest, upright, lovable, kind, compassionate person who had once been a horrible, hateful, despicable, gutter drunk. To see that degenerate character transformed into a saint would rejoice the heart of God. But the *amazing grace* that brings to our ears so sweet a sound is how God could love the unlovely sinner who is dead, deteriorating, rotting in sin.

Perhaps you do not particularly like the expression, "rotting in sin." Suppose we allow the Holy Spirit to describe the unregenerate:

"FOR FROM WITHIN, OUT OF THE HEART OF MEN (unregenerated men), PROCEED:

Evil thoughts,

Adulteries,

Fornications,

Murders,

Thefts,

Covetousness,

Wickedness,

Deceit,

Lasciviousness,

An evil eye,

Blasphemy,

Pride,

Foolishness:

ALL THESE EVIL THINGS COME FROM WITHIN, AND DEFILE THE MAN" (Mark 7:21–23).

If that Scripture does not prove to you that within every unregenerated person there is a potential spiritual garbage can, hear this:

"The heart is deceitful above all things, and desperately wicked: who can know it?" (Jeremiah 17:9).

Every unregenerated person reading these lines has within his bosom a heart that is capable of manufacturing, producing, and delivering any one of the evils catalogued in Mark 7:21–23. The only way to guarantee yourself that you will not practice these evils is to submit your heart to God and let Him remove that heart by the operation of the Holy Ghost and put a brand new heart in its place!

Is that possible? We will look in our Textbook to find out:

"A NEW HEART also will I give you, AND A NEW SPIRIT will I put within you: and I will take away THE STONY HEART out of your flesh, and I WILL GIVE YOU A NEW HEART" (Ezek. 36:26).

3. *Grace*: The age-old definition of Grace, accepted by most believers, is simply "God's unmerited favor." Of course, that is a very limited definition of Grace. Read the account of the sufferings of Jesus in the Prophets, the Psalms and the Gospels——and then:

"For the Law was given by Moses, BUT GRACE AND TRUTH came by Jesus Christ" (John 1:17). Grace is "the kindness and love of God our Saviour toward men . . . not by works of righteousness which we have done" (Titus 3:4–5). Grace therefore is constantly set in the Scriptures in contrast to the Law of Moses. Under the Law of Moses, God demands righteousness from man. But under Grace, God in Christ *gives* righteousness TO man (study Rom. 3:21–22, Rom. 8:4, Rom. 10:4, Phil. 3:9, Rom. 3:20).

The Law came by Moses; the Law is connected with Moses and with works. Grace came by Jesus Christ—— yea, Grace WAS Jesus Christ——and becomes ours by faith (John 1:17, Rom. 10:4–10, Eph. 2:8–9, Titus 2:11). The Law extends blessings to the good——but Grace extends salvation to the bad . . . yea, to the worst. (Study Exodus 19:5, Eph. 2:1–9, Titus 2:11–15.) The Law demands that blessings be earned by righteous works; but Grace is the free gift of God, no strings attached. By Grace . . . the gift of God. (Study Deut. 28:1–6, Eph. 2:8, Rom. 4:4–5.)

The Dispensation of Grace began with the death and

resurrection of the Lord Jesus. (Study Rom. 3:24—26 and Rom. 4:24—25.) Since the cross, salvation does not depend upon religious practices such as rituals, feasts, the keeping of Sabbaths, assemblies, etc. Salvation depends upon receiving Jesus. In this dispensation we are saved or lost because we receive or reject Jesus. Good works have nothing to do with salvation. Good works are the evidence, the fruit, of salvation. (Study carefully John 1:12—13, John 3:36, John 5:24, Matt. 21:37, Matt. 22:42, John 15:22—25, Heb. 1:1—3, I John 5:10—12.)

No person has ever been saved by keeping the Law. The only person who ever kept the Law was the Lord Jesus Christ (Matt. 5:17, John 17). No one except Jesus ever kept God's Law perfectly——and God's Law demands perfection. If we break the least, we are guilty of all. The Law of God was not given to save people: "Therefore, by the deeds of the Law there shall no flesh be justified" (Rom. 3:20). The Law demands a certain standard of conduct . . . a standard that must conform to God's righteous requirements for man; and when man oversteps these requirements he is automatically a sinner, an enemy to God. ALL men have overstepped the requirements of the Law.

The Law condemns man because of his inability to live up to the requirements of the Law. However, the Grace of God on the other hand provides and meets the needs of man. Grace provides the righteousness which God's righteousness requires under Law. Grace provides what Law could never have provided. The Law was weak through the flesh (Rom. 8:1—3). But God the Father made Christ the Son to be sin for us (II Cor. 5:21) in order that we in Jesus might be made the righteousness of God. When we are justified by faith we are just as just as Jesus is just in the sight of God Almighty. We are just as pure as the blood that covers us. We are just as righteous as the divine nature that abides within (II Peter 1:4). On the grounds and basis of the righteousness provided by the Grace of God, God sets aside man's just deserts . . . He overlooks man's demerit and ill desert as though man had never sinned. It is not the merit of man that makes us acceptable unto God, but the merit of the God-Man, Jesus in flesh. Because death could not hold Him He is able to save to the uttermost all who come to God by Him. When we are saved we are placed in Christ, we become holy because He is holy (Col. 1:27, Col. 3:3, Gal. 2:20). The natural man is dead in sins, disobedient to the holy God, thereby deserving God's wrath. The natural man is not able to correct his ill conduct toward God, he is not able to do anything about his just desert from a holy God; therefore the natural man finds himself in darkness and despair——helpless, hopeless, and hell-bound. "BUT GOD . . ." in His mercy and love did something about it. God has wholly corrected and provided a way of escape by His mercy, His love, and His grace. God's mercy, God's love, and God's grace are the sole source and secret of our glorious salvation.

God is a "CONSUMING FIRE" (Heb. 12:29), but God is also a God of "LOVING KINDNESS AND TENDER MERCIES."

THE RESULTS OF GOD'S MERCY, LOVE AND GRACE

1. In Christ we are now raised from the dead.

As a result of God's great mercy, lovingkindness and gracious Grace, we who believe are raised from the deadness of sin. Thank God, it is past tense: "RAISED!" We are not *going to be* raised, we are not *being* raised. Salvation is not future tense, nor is it progressive, in parts, nor on the installment plan. We are resurrected from the dead instantaneously, the split second we embrace the finished work of Jesus by faith.

Because of God's Grace (Heb. 2:9) Jesus was permitted to taste death for every man. To fully appreciate the deep spiritual truth taught here, we must study again Romans 6:1ff. We——each and every one of us——deserved death and hell, because all have sinned; but He (God), for us and for our sake, counted His only begotten Son worthy of death. Judicially Jesus died our death and we died with Him: *"We are dead*——and our lives are hid with Christ in God" (Col. 3:3). In the same manner, we are raised with Him . . . not *going to be*, but we are NOW raised with Him. The true believer is just as sure for heaven as Jesus is sure for heaven——and He is there! Positionally we sit with Him NOW. I know that is too glorious for human comprehension. I confess that I do not understand it; but I believe it because it is pure Scripture without the taint of man's thinking, reason, speculation or exegesis. Jesus died, He was buried, and He rose again.

Christian baptism is for believers only——and if you have not been baptized since you believed you have not had Christian baptism. Christian baptism is an ordinance of the New Testament church signifying that we have died with Jesus, are buried with Him and raised to walk in newness of life. Water baptism does not save us, water baptism does not wash away our sins, water baptism has nothing to do with redemption. But we should be baptized in obedience, in order to fulfill all righteous acts. We cannot partake of righteous acts until after we have been made righteous in Jesus, through the redemption that is in His blood, received on our part by faith.

Jesus died, was buried, and rose again; and when we receive His finished work we die and are raised with Him. "I am crucified with Christ (crucifixion means death):

84

nevertheless I live (I was crucified when Jesus was crucified, but I am alive now); yet not I, but Christ liveth in me: and the life which I now live in the flesh I live by the faith of the Son of God, who loved me, and gave Himself for me" (Gal. 2:20). Please study carefully Col. 2:20 and Col. 3:4. Also study Rom. 6:8–13.

2. With Christ we are now seated in the heavenlies.

Jesus died, was buried, rose again, appeared to the believers, was taken up into glory and He is coming again. (Study the entire fifteenth chapter of I Corinthians.)

In Jesus we died, we were buried, we are now risen, and we are NOW (present tense) seated with Jesus——IN Jesus——at the right hand of God the Father. Beloved, I do not profess to understand it——but I dare not refuse to believe it because the Holy Spirit has revealed this glorious fact to this unworthy heart of mine. The Holy Spirit has planted in my bosom this abounding, astounding, astonishing assurance. Did I hear you say, "I cannot accept it . . . I cannot believe it" . . . is that what you said? If you did, then kind friend, perhaps you had better check up and see if you have had a change of heart, because it is the natural man who refuses to believe the things of the Spirit. The born again receive the things of the Spirit because He (the Spirit) is the teacher of the Word. He moved upon holy men, they penned down God's message——and since the Holy Spirit is the author of the Bible He is very capable of teaching us——yea, even the deep things of God.

Those who deny the mystical body of Christ (the Invisible Church) cannot comprehend nor accept what I have just said. But we know that the church IS His body . . . we know He is the head and the Foundation, we are members of His body, and positionally we are seated with the Head of the church. "In Him" we actually are seated in the heavenlies. What a contrast from that which we were before we became believers!

3. *In Christ we have a glorious future.*

"(God) hath raised us up together, and made us sit together in heavenly places in Christ Jesus" for a singular reason:

"That in the ages (the eternity) to come He might shew the exceeding riches of His grace in His kindness toward us through Christ Jesus." God is going to display the exceeding riches of His Grace in His kindness toward us. This is a future tense benefit of our redemption. We are raised (now——present tense)——we do sit (now) with Jesus in the heavenlies——but we *will be* placed on display in the heavenlies in the ages to come. This glorious fact (or benefit) of redemption is foreign to most Christians . . . they are totally ignorant of it.

In that grand and glorious day when Jesus is manifested in power and great glory, we (the church, the Bride) will occupy the Pearly White City which is now being prepared for us (John 14:1–6, Rev. 21:1–27). Revelation 21:9 tells us: "And there came unto me one of the seven angels which had the seven vials full of the seven last plagues, and talked with me, saying, Come hither, I will shew thee the bride, the Lamb's wife." Then it was that John was carried into a great high mountain and He saw the Holy Jerusalem, the Pearly White City, descending from God out of Heaven. That Pearly White City is the place to which Jesus was referring when He said, "In my Father's house are many mansions . . . I go to prepare a place for *you*." The place being prepared for the Bride (the church) is the Pearly White City.

There are three heavens mentioned in the Scripture. In II Corinthians 12:1–3 Paul distinctly refers to the *third* heaven. If there is a third heaven there must of necessity be heaven number one and heaven number two. The first heaven is where the clouds are. The second heaven is where the planets and the constellations are. The third heaven is God's house——Paradise. We will have a new heaven, a new earth——and the Pearly White City.

The new heaven is the atmospheric heavens just above us that will be delivered——the demons will be removed and put into hell and the prince of the power of the air will be cast into the bottomless pit. We will have a new first heaven.

The second heaven will be renovated——all the stars and planets will fall, the moon will drip with blood, the sun will be needed no more for Jesus will be the light of God's new creation.

The Pearly White City will be suspended between God's house and the new earth, and it will be the home of the church . . . all who are saved by God's marvelous grace. All of God's creation——the peoples on the new earth, the angels in heaven (God's house)——will see the Pearly White City, and will witness throughout eternity the display of the exceeding riches of God's grace that brought about the Bride, the Lamb's wife. So . . . this glorious event lies ahead in the ages to come.

In Ephesians 2:8—10 we have the origin and the outcome of salvation . . . by grace, through faith, ye are saved . . . it is the gift of God, not yourselves. We have the certainty of salvation: "Ye ARE saved!" We have the fact clearly set forth that salvation IS God's gift . . . man has nothing to do with redemption. Greek scholars tell us that the words "it is" are not found in the Greek text. Ephesians 2:8 should read "For by grace are ye saved through faith; and that not of yourselves: the gift of God."

I trust you will accept the statement I am going to make, because I have scripture to back it up: Salvation is totally and entirely (one hundred percent in every minute detail) *of God, through* God, the *gift* of God. Not one iota of anything that man can do, be, say or give adds one mite, one jot or tittle, to God's redemption. Here is what I mean: We are saved by grace. Grace is God's unmerited favor. Grace provides for us what we do not deserve. Grace does the saving; but Grace becomes ours by faith. We exercise the faith——but how do we exercise the faith, why do we exercise the faith? Where do we get the faith? ". . . FAITH COMETH BY HEARING, AND HEARING BY THE WORD OF GOD" (Rom. 10:17). So you see, God Almighty in the beginning perfected salvation, completed salvation, and in the fulness of time presented salvation. All you or I can do to become the recipient of salvation is to hear the Gospel, and receive Jesus through the faith brought to our heart by hearing the Gospel. It is all of God, beloved. I have been preaching the Gospel for many years, and the hardest thing on this earth for me to get across to people is the Bible fact that man cannot save himself——nor can man help God save him. Salvation is totally and entirely of God.

Ephesians 2:10 tells us that "we are His workmanship, created in Christ Jesus." We who are saved are the products of God's marvelous grace. We are not what we are through any work, labor or merit on our part. We are the workmanship of God, we are the product of God's works.

Christians are not manufactured from other products to make us better persons. We are "CREATED" . . . not educated, not trained, not cultured, not overhauled, repaired, or put in first-class condition; we are "CREATED." Today thousands of preachers are substituting education for regeneration; religion for repentance; works for grace; but "except a man be born from above he cannot see the kingdom of God." The natural man must be created in Christ Jesus, thereby becoming a new creation. This happens by the provision and the operation of the grace of our God.

The first man (Adam) became a dead sinner because of disobedience. The second Adam (Christ Jesus) became flesh, and in the flesh did what the first Adam failed to do . . . He conquered the world, the flesh and the devil, death, hell and the grave. Therefore, "If any man be in Christ Jesus he is a new creature" (II Cor. 5:17). God does not repair natural man . . . God creates a new man within. A person who is truly born of the Spirit, regenerated by the power of God, saved by the grace of God, is THE MASTERPIECE OF ALL GOD'S CREATIVE ACTS.

Salvation is not OF works, but salvation is "unto good works." By our good works we prove to ourselves and to our fellowman that we are saved. James declares, "As the body without the spirit is dead, so faith without works is dead also" (James 2:26). It is not the quantity of works (how *much* you do) that proves you are saved, but the fact that good works automatically follow salvation. The believers at Thessalonica proved their salvation by turning to God from idols, to *serve* God (I Thess. 1:9). The Ephesian believers confessed, brought their books of magic and burned them before all the people, thereby proving that they had experienced a change of heart (Acts 19:18—20). The believers at Rome who were the servants of sin, obeyed from the heart the doctrine of salvation by grace through faith, and they became the servants of righteousness unto holiness (Rom. 6:14—23). Works have nothing to do with redemption; but works testify that redemption has been wrought in the heart. We work because we are the sons of God. We do not work to try to gain heaven——we work because we are on the way *to* heaven. Salvation is totally and entirely by Grace, the gift of God. Our eternal reward will be determined by our faithful works . . . our faithful stewardship. (Study carefully I Corinthians 3:11–15.)

Let me share with you a truth the Holy Spirit has just revealed to me as I study and ponder these messages: So far as our redemption is concerned, spiritually we are *sitting*. For example, in Hebrews 1:1–3 we read, "God, who at sundry times and in divers manners spake in time past unto the fathers by the prophets, hath in these last days spoken unto us by His Son, whom He hath appointed heir of all things, by whom also He made the worlds; Who being the brightness of His glory, and the express image of His person, and upholding all things by the word of His power, WHEN HE HAD BY HIMSELF PURGED OUR SINS, SAT DOWN on the right hand of the Majesty on high." (Note: When Jesus had completed redemption, He took a seat. He had finished the work God sent Him to do.) In this Scripture we clearly see that Jesus finished every minute detail of redemption according to God's blueprint and plan. And when He had finished redemption He sat down . . . and to me that signifies a man after a hard day on the farm, in the shop, in the plant . . . when the day is finished he goes to the warmth, shelter and security of the home . . . and he sits down. When Jesus had paid sin's debt He sat down at God's right hand. He had finished redemption. Nothing can be added by God or man so far as the saving of the soul is concerned. When we trust Jesus our redemption is complete . . . finished. The split second we are born into God's family, we are as much a son of God as we will ever be. We are completely and totally redeemed. We are taken out of the slave market of sin and placed into the family of God–– no longer a slave, but a son.

When a new-born babe comes to the home, the moment

it is born it is a son . . . it is a body——not full grown, but a living personality, a complete body. The same is true in redemption: We become a son of God by faith in the finished work of Jesus, and when we are saved (so far as redemption is concerned) we sit down to rest in the heavenlies with Jesus until that glorious day when we will receive our glorified body to reign with Jesus. So now, those of us who are born again are resting . . . we are sitting with Jesus so far as redemption is concerned. But notice: We are walking here on earth. The inner man, the spirit, is sitting with Jesus in heavenly places; but we are walking on earth . . . a pilgrim, a stranger. We are His workmanship, we are created in Christ Jesus unto good works. God hath before ordained "THAT WE SHOULD WALK IN THEM." The believer is forever on the move, never still, always walking for Jesus. "Whether therefore you eat or drink——or whatsoever you do——do all to the glory of God." That is the reason Paul cried out, "I beseech you (I beg you) to present your bodies a living sacrifice!" (Rom. 12:1). "Yield your members as instruments of righteousness!" (Rom. 6:13). We should be walking daily, working daily, in such manner that others might see our walk and our works, and glorify God because of the display of the miracle of grace in our lives!

God the Son is seated beside God the Father in heaven——but God the Holy Spirit is walking on earth . . . convicting sinners, drawing sinners to God; indwelling and assuring believers; leading believers in the paths of righteousness for the name's sake of Jesus. In Ephesians 2:6 *we sit with Jesus*. In Ephesians 2:10 *we walk with the Holy Spirit*. ". . . WALK IN THE SPIRIT AND YE SHALL NOT FULFIL THE LUST OF THE FLESH" (Galatians 5:16).

THE BLOOD OF JESUS CHRIST THE SON OF GOD
BREAKS DOWN RACIAL BARRIERS

Verses 11–13: "Wherefore remember, that ye being in time past Gentiles in the flesh, who are called Uncircumcision by that which is called the Circumcision in the flesh made by hands; that at that time ye were without Christ, being aliens from the commonwealth of Israel, and strangers from the covenants of promise, having no hope, and without God in the world: But now in Christ Jesus ye who sometimes were far off are made nigh by the blood of Christ."

Up to verse 11 we have dealt with individuals—either as sinners, or as sons . . . saved, or lost. But here we pass into a deeper truth: We see clearly that the blood of Jesus Christ breaks down all racial barriers . . . Jew and Gentile become one in the body of Christ. Certainly the blood of Jesus Christ saves the individual, and salvation is an individual act; but it goes beyond that.

Jesus certainly died for the individual—but His command is, "the Gospel to every creature" . . . Jew, Gentile, rich, poor, bond or free. He "hath made of one blood all nations of men." *In Christ* we have a new society. I know of no chapter in the Bible that more clearly points out the grace of God to all people than does John chapter four. Study the entire chapter. The Samaritan woman met Jesus at the well, and He asked her for a drink. She could not understand His being a Jew—yet asking a Samaritan woman for a drink. Jesus said to her, "If thou knewest . . . who it is that saith to thee, Give me to drink; thou wouldest have asked of Him, and He would have given thee living water."

The beautiful picture of salvation continues here, until the woman who came to the well, bringing an empty water pot, returned to the city with wells of living water flowing forth from her innermost being. So . . . in this marvelous Dispensation of the Grace of God, it is no longer Jew or Gentile: It is ALL nations, one in Christ . . . that is, *all who believe*. There is no difference.

Paul reminds the believers at Ephesus (and you and me, and all other Gentiles) that in time past we were strangers to God's covenant, aliens from the elect nation Israel. We were Gentile "dogs." Even the disciples were instructed to go to the lost sheep of the house of Israel and were commanded NOT to go into the way of the Gentiles. The same command was given to the seventy; and when the Syrophenician woman (a Gentile) came to Jesus He informed her that the bread was for the children, not for dogs. The woman recognized the fact that she was a Gentile, and she reminded the Master that even the dogs eat the crumbs that fall from the children's table. The literal translation from the Greek in this particular verse is "the little dogs . . . or, the puppies"; and this dear woman, for the sake of her daughter, was willing to take a puppy's place to receive the blessing from the Lord Jesus, the Lamb of God. Jesus told her in so many words, "Because of your faith, heaven is at your disposal" (Matt. 15:22—28).

Yes, Paul reminds us that we were Gentiles in the flesh, we belonged to the great mass of lost, hell-bound humanity. Whether a small tribe in a remote jungle, or a giant nation in the flourishing cities, ALL natural men upon the face of the earth corrupt themselves with lust, immoralities, and the things of the devil. Without God and the miracle of His grace, the individual, the tribe, or the nation follows the flesh and dies IN the flesh, eternally lost!

According to Romans chapter one and Romans 2:1, we

know that all men are inexcusable in their ignorance of God. There is no excuse, because our first parents (Adam and Eve) knew God and later Noah and his family (the only living souls on this earth) knew God. But as men multiplied they refused to glorify God AS God. They changed the truth of God into a lie. They did not like to retain God in their knowledge; therefore they became darkened in their intelligence, depraved in their souls. Read Romans 1:21—32 and you will find a sad catalog of sins that brought multiplied millions of heathen into existence upon this earth.

In Ephesians 2:11 the Jews referred to the Gentiles as "the uncircumcision." They regarded Gentiles as entirely outside the mercy of God, without any right, any hope or standing. Spiritually they were to them as "dogs." But Paul uses a phrase that lowers the Jews to much the same level:

While the Gentiles were "Gentiles in the flesh," the Jew deserves to be called *"circumcision in the flesh* made by hands." This was a mere cutting of the flesh, and the ritual had lost its spiritual import of the symbol of circumcision about the heart, to effect a separation unto God.

If you will take into consideration the statement Paul makes here to the Gentiles, in a city where there were also Jews other than himself, you will see that he was a preacher with a backbone. He put the Jews in the same category with the "Gentile dogs." Oh, yes——the unregenerate Ephesians were Gentiles in the flesh, but Paul declares here that we are ALL (Jew or Gentile, bond or free) in the same category. Read Romans chapter 3 very carefully.

In Paul's day, the Jew was very bitter toward the Gentile; but Paul warned the Jews that their formalism which did not change the heart nor add righteousness to the inner man, was the thing that caused racial hatred. The Jews refused to hear Jesus when He announced that He had come to save sinners . . . Jew, Gentile, or whomsoever. The racial bigotry and race hatred in the heart of the Jew rejected their Messiah, refused to accept the Gentile as a brother, and finally nailed their Christ to a cross!

In our present passage of Scripture Paul tells us that we were "without God in the world." Yes, we were without *God*, and we were also *without* (on the outside) so far as the Jew who professed to know God was concerned. He refused to reach out his hand to the Gentile dog and say, "Come, my friend, into the family of God!" Instead, he refused to have any dealings with the Gentiles, and it is said that the Jew prayed at the beginning of the day that God would deliver him from seeing the face of a Gentile. I suppose there is no hatred on earth today quite so deep as the hatred the Jew had for the Gentile when Jesus came into the world to pay the sin-debt. But Paul tells us in Romans that "through their fall salvation is come to the Gentiles." God can bring blessing out of tragedy.

We were definitely out . . . we had more than three strikes against us. We were without Christ, the Messiah who came to the lost sheep of the house of Israel, we were without a place among God's covenant people, alienated from the nation to which God gave the Law, and to whom He had sent Jesus, their king. We were strangers to His covenants of promise. God had pledged Himself to Israel, had given His promise to Abraham, and God could not and would not break His word. As Gentiles we were without God in the world, having many gods, but only gods who do not hear and speak . . . gods who could not help us. Yes, we Gentiles who are members of the body of Christ should shout the praises of God because of His grace which permitted Jesus Christ to taste death for Gentile "dogs."

I am so thankful today that I can tell ALL men--regardless of their race, regardless of their social standing--that Jesus died on the cross for the sins of the whole wide world! Up to His death, the message was to the lost sheep of the house of Israel; but in John 10:16 Jesus said, "Other sheep I have, which are not of this fold." He declared that He would make all sheep ONE fold. Up to the crucifixion, Jesus had a flock of sheep made up only of Israelites; but on this side of the cross, the "other sheep" have been incorporated into the fold of God, and now there is ONE FOLD made up of Jews, Gentiles . . . and "whosoever will."

The miracle of the one fold is summed up in three words: the "BLOOD OF CHRIST." "BUT NOW IN CHRIST JESUS YE WHO SOMETIMES WERE FAR OFF ARE MADE NIGH BY THE BLOOD OF CHRIST."

Through the inspired pen of Paul the Holy Spirit sets forth this inescapable contrast: "In times past . . . at that time . . . BUT NOW . . . ." Again, "We WERE . . . BUT NOW . . . we ARE!" We clearly see what we were as Gentiles, alienated from God, and we see what we are "in Christ."

There was only one way known to God . . . it HAD to be *by the blood of Christ.*" Even Jehovah God could provide no other way:

"When I see the blood, I will pass over you."

"Without the shedding of blood is no remission."

"The blood of Jesus Christ, God's Son, cleanseth us from all sin."

"Ye were not redeemed with corruptible things such as silver and gold . . . but with the precious blood of

Christ as of a lamb without spot or blemish."

All born again believers are blood kin . . . brothers and sisters because we are all under the blood of the Lord Jesus. Through the power of the blood we are all in Christ, one family, blood-bought and blood-related to God. We were purchased by the blood of God (Acts 20:28).

IN CHRIST WE HAVE PEACE

Verses 14—18: "For He is our peace, who hath made both one, and hath broken down the middle wall of partition between us; having abolished in His flesh the enmity, even the law of commandments contained in ordinances; for to make in Himself of twain one NEW MAN, so making peace; and that He might reconcile both unto God in ONE BODY by the cross, having slain the enmity thereby: and came and preached peace to you which were afar off, and to them that were nigh. For through Him we both have access by one Spirit unto the Father."

You will notice the word "peace" is used three times in this short portion of our study. In the Old Testament the peace offering must be "without blemish" (Lev. 3:1). Certainly Jesus, our peace offering to God, was without blemish. He was an offering that God could and did accept. In the Old Testament, the peace offering was "an offering made by fire unto Jehovah" (Lev. 3:3). Of course, the fire was a picture of the wrath of God upon sin. Jesus went through the fire for us. I do not mean that He literally burned in hell——no, certainly not; but He suffered every pain and all the agony that an eternal hell affords. He took the sinner's place. Before He left this world, He said, "Peace I leave with you, my peace I give unto you: not as the world giveth, give I unto you. Let not your heart be troubled, neither let it be afraid" (John 14:27). The result of the cross is peace for both Jew and

Gentile, because by the death of Jesus on the cross, He "hath broken down the middle wall of partition." This refers to the temple's outer court which was for Gentiles, separated from the inner court into which only the Jew dared enter. But now, in this marvelous day of grace since Calvary, "CHRIST IS THE END OF THE LAW FOR RIGHTEOUSNESS TO EVERY ONE THAT BELIEVETH" (Rom. 10:4). Through His blood He has "abolished in His flesh the enmity, even the law of commandments contained in ordinances."

Note these precious words of truth: "For in Him dwelleth all the fulness of the Godhead bodily. And ye are complete in Him, which is the head of all principality and power: in whom also ye (Gentiles) are circumcised with the circumcision made without hands, in putting off the body of the sins of the flesh by the circumcision of Christ: Buried with Him in baptism, wherein also ye are risen with Him through the faith of the operation of God, who hath raised Him from the dead. And you, being dead in your sins and the uncircumcision of your flesh, hath He quickened together with Him, having forgiven you all trespasses; BLOTTING OUT the handwriting of ordinances that was against us, which was contrary to us, and took it out of the way, NAILING IT TO HIS CROSS; And having spoiled principalities and powers, He made a shew of them openly, triumphing over them in it. Let no man therefore judge you in meat, or in drink, or in respect of an holyday, or of the new moon, or of the sabbath days: WHICH ARE A SHADOW OF THINGS TO COME; BUT THE BODY IS OF CHRIST" (Col. 2:9—17).

JESUS LEFT THE FATHER'S BOSOM AND CAME TO EARTH'S SORROWS . . . "to make in Himself of twain one *new man*." This——and only this, is the solution to the problem of sin, bigotry and hatred among the peoples of earth, regardless of what governments try to do to wipe out race hatred, religious hatred, and bigotry. The governments of earth will never solve the problem. There is only one solution: The grace of God in hearts, creating within the heart a *new man*. When this happens, regardless of color, race or whatsoever, brothers and sisters in Christ will love one another. Jesus did not come into the world to patch up the old creation by cleaning up slums, building superhighways, colleges and universities. Jesus did not come to patch up the old nature. God's wisdom knew that this could never solve the problem of sin, and in His wisdom He provided the Lord Jesus, that through His sacrifice——His shed blood on the cross—— Gentiles and Jews, rich and poor, bond and free, could be made one new creation in Christ (II Cor. 5:17). True love one for another is not the result of an outward experience ——but of an inward miracle through the grace of God.

See this word-picture of the unregenerated heart: "For we ourselves (that includes Paul) also were sometimes foolish, disobedient, deceived, serving divers lusts and pleasures, *living in malice and envy, hateful, and hating one another.* BUT . . . after that the kindness of the love of God our Saviour toward man appeared, Not by works of righteousness which we have done, but according to His mercy He saved us, by the washing of regeneration, and renewing of the Holy Ghost; which He shed on us abundantly through Jesus Christ our Saviour; That being justified by His grace, we should be made heirs according to the hope of eternal life" (Titus 3:3–7).

So . . . according to the Apostle Paul, all sinners (some more than others) are foolish, disobedient, deceived. They serve all kinds of lusts and pleasures, and they live in malice and envy. They are hateful——and they hate one another. Let us not be deceived, beloved: The unregenerate heart is a spiritual garbage can! The only way to get rid of the garbage is to get rid of the can . . . the old heart . . . and let God through the miracle of the operation of the Holy Ghost put a new heart in your bosom––because it is from the heart that the issues of life proceed. We MUST have a change of heart before we can live right, think right, act right, be right . . . and love right. I say this humbly––but I make no apology for saying it: An unsaved person does not know the meaning of real love. No person can love in the deeper sense until God, by faith, abides in the heart . . . because "God is love."

The Age of Grace is not the old order repaired, nor a better day. This Day of Grace is a new day. Former things are set aside (Col. 2:9–17). Believers are partakers of God's life and nature. We are led by a Person . . . the Holy Spirit within. True believers live in harmony, in loving accord, because we are members of one body. There is a day coming when there will be peace on earth––not just among individuals, but the whole earth will be at peace one with another. Good will among men will be everywhere. But that will only be when Jesus sits on the throne in Jerusalem, and the knowledge of the Lord covers this earth as the waters now cover the sea. All of this is made possible *by the cross*. There He gave His body in sacrifice, that from its poured-out life He might form a new body. Jesus suffered "in His flesh," that He might meet God in the flesh and satisfy the demand of God's holiness in a body like unto your body and mine, that He might reconcile to God Jew and Gentile . . . every race and every man . . . regardless of his position or condition. Jesus has "slain the enmity." This came about only because Jesus took a body like unto the body possessed by the men who, through envy, delivered Him up to Pilate to be crucified. Therefore, He who was slain by the enmity of wicked men, has in turn slain the enmity that existed between a holy God and sinful men.

Jesus preached peace . . . peace to the Jew and peace to the Gentile. An angel announced the birth of Jesus by proclaiming, "Behold, I bring you good tidings of great joy . . . for unto you is born this day in the city of David, a Saviour . . . ." The heavenly host announced good tidings, great joy, a Saviour, peace on earth, and good will toward men (Luke 2:10–14).

When Jesus came as a babe in a manger nineteen-hundred years ago, He came to die (Heb. 2:9 and 14). He came to seek and to save that which was lost (Luke 19:10). He came to lay His life down (John 10:17–18), a ransom for many. He died on the cross, laid down His life for sinners. They crucified Him and buried Him; but the grave could not hold Him. He arose, ascended back to the Father, and sent the Holy Spirit as He had promised His disciples. The Holy Spirit now abides in the bosom of every born again child of God. Today every believer belongs to one body, baptized into that body by one Spirit (I Cor. 12:13). As individual believers, we should be busy going to every creature in obedience to the command, "Preach the Gospel of peace, and bring glad tidings of good things" (Rom. 10:15).

The world's need at this solemn, crucial, dangerous hour is not guided missiles, nor man in outer space. The answer to the ills of the peoples of earth is found in the message of the Gospel: *Peace and glad tidings.* But the sad thing is that we in America are spending billions of dollars to put a man on the moon——while we give only pennies to win men to Christ!

Perhaps someone is asking, "Has the mission of Jesus to earth failed?" Perhaps you are suggesting that there is no peace on earth today. This is the age of wholesale slaughter. Every nation under heaven is making a mad rush to invent and manufacture a bomb that will kill the most people for the least invested. But beloved, let me remind you that those of us who "study to show ourselves approved unto God" (II Tim. 2:15) know that THIS IS NOT THE HOUR OF THE PRINCE OF PEACE. Read Matthew chapter ten, and you will discover that Jesus said, "Think not that I have come to bring peace on earth . . . I came not to bring peace, but a sword." This is not the hour of the Prince of Peace; His hour is just ahead of us. This is man's day . . . next comes HIS day. We are warned, "For when they shall say, PEACE AND SAFETY (are not the front pages of our newspapers filled with such propaganda?) then sudden destruction cometh upon them, as travail upon a woman with child; and they shall not escape" (I Thess. 5:3).

The failure of man is inevitable. It is in evidence all around us. God knows the end in the beginning, and He has provided that day of peace; but it will only come when God has put all enemies under the feet of His beloved Son! At this particular time, the Holy Ghost is calling out a people . . . Jew and Gentile . . . (a people made up of all races, all nations, all classes) who are known as the church, the body of Christ. When this body is completed the church will be caught up into the clouds in the air to meet Jesus (I Thess. 4:13–18). Then God will deal with the wicked on earth, and after that we will have that grand and glorious day of peace! However, never forget that the Person and the work of the Lord Jesus Christ are the center, the heart, the soul, the very essence of the whole Christian program of God. Jesus is our peace. He made peace, He brought peace, and He gives peace *now* to the individual who believes in Him. When He comes again there will be "peace on earth."

While on this earth, the Lord Jesus backed up every thing He said, by the things He did. Had it been possible for the devil to stop Jesus before He reached the cross, the entire program of Christianity would have fallen apart, because it was imperative that Jesus die on a cross. This truth is set forth in His own words: "And I, if I be lifted up from the earth, will draw all men unto me" (John 12:32). It was an eternal necessity that Jesus die on the cross. The blood of Jesus is the essence of God's requirement in answer to the demands of God's law. The offering had to be the sin-less offering provided by a sin-less person, "AS OF THE LAMB WITHOUT BLEMISH AND WITHOUT SPOT." You may be asking, "Why?" The answer: The very nature of a holy God, separate from sin, could not accept any offering less than a sin-less offering. Sin had separated man from God, and had created a great gulf between God and man. The only way this great separating gulf could be removed was through the sacrifice of a sin-less offering.

The Epistles of Paul are a continuation of truth . . . truth that begins in the Gospels, words uttered by Him who said, "I am the Truth." But truths that go deeper and become more precious in the epistles, when we see and lay hold on the fact that in the Person and work of the Lord Jesus we are not only reconciled TO God, but we become a partaker of the life of God, and we are one with Him in Christ. The blood that ran from the veins of the Lord Jesus, the blood that covered His face as it ran from His thorn-pierced brow——that blood has sufficed to form a new body in which all believers are incorporated and made one——yea, one person: *Christ.* He is the head, we are the body (Eph. 5:30). Tremendous? Yes. Past human wisdom and understanding? Yes. Nevertheless—— Bible truth.

Speaking to the Colossians (referring to believers in the church), Paul said, "And have put on the new man, which is renewed in knowledge after the image of Him that CREATED HIM: where there is neither Greek nor

Jew, circumcision nor uncircumcision, Barbarian, Scythian, bond nor free: *but Christ is all, and in all*" (Col. 3:10—11).

In these words we have revealed the very heart and secret . . . the very essence . . . of the Christian system. The grace of God does not make one a better man; grace creates a *new* man belonging to another order . . . a brand new family, a new creation.

Verse 18 in our present passage leads us a step further: Through Him (Jesus) we both have access by one Spirit unto the Father. All born again believers, regardless of race, have access through the Lord Jesus——the Mediator of the new covenant. It was Jesus who "suffered for sins, the just for the unjust, that He might bring us to God" (I Peter 3:18). It was Jesus who said, "No man cometh to the Father but by me" (John 14:6). It was Jesus who said, "He that climbeth up some other way, the same is a thief and a robber" (John 10:1). It was Jesus who said, "And ye will not come to me that ye might have life" (John 5:39—40).

Keep in mind the fact that all spiritual blessings are *IN Christ Jesus*. Redemption has been wrought for us *in Christ Jesus*. The Spirit works in us, the Spirit possesses the regenerated heart. The Spirit is the power that lives daily in us. The new man, whether he be Jew or Gentile, is led by the Holy Spirit.

The proof of Christianity is not found in theology or ethics——but in the new man created by Christianity . . . and Jesus Christ IS Christianity. The life lived in Christ is the proof that Christianity is right and every other religion on this earth is man-made. "There is a way that seemeth right unto a man, but the end thereof are the ways of death" (Prov. 16:25).

There is one God . . . we believe that. Most religions

104

acknowledge that fact——but there is also ONE Mediator between God and men: "THE MAN CHRIST JESUS" (I Tim. 2:5). The only One who can mediate between God and the believer is the Lord Jesus Christ.

Can the place be found in God's holy Word where the believer is invited to intercede in prayer to Peter or to some other saint? Can it be found in holy writ where we are to consult saints for the privilege of talking to God? Is it found in the Bible that believers are to request the mother of Jesus to plead our case? You know the an-swer——NO! There is but One to whom God listens. God the Father hears mediation from the Son, on behalf of the saint (who became a saint because of simple faith in the shed blood of Jesus Christ). In this marvelous Dispen-sation of the Grace of God, we are all kings, priests and saints——and the least believer, the most insignificant per-son, is invited boldly into the holy of holies by a new and living way . . . through the body (the death) of the Lord Jesus Christ. (Study I Peter 2:9 and Heb. 10:19–20.) There is no other name given under heaven among men whereby we must be saved. There is one Mediator be-tween God and men——the Man Christ Jesus. He who climbs up some other way, the same is a thief and a rob-ber. Jesus is the Way, the Truth, the Life. No man com-eth unto the Father but by Jesus. The entrance to heaven is singular——the Man, Christ Jesus. The Intercessor be-tween God and men is singular——the Man, Christ Jesus. All spiritual blessings become ours through a singular avenue——the Man, Christ Jesus. When we enter the por-tals of glory it will be because the Man, Christ Jesus, confesses us to the Heavenly Father. Do not let anyone rob you of the right to eternal life by preaching to you that there is some other way. Remember——the devil is transformed as an angel of light, and his ministers are transformed as ministers of righteousness——but their end will be according to their damnable heresies. Just as surely as God has called Spirit-filled, ordained ministers, the devil also has called demonized ministers. (Study carefully II Cor. 11:13–15.) Beware of wolves in sheep's clothing! The dirtiest thief this side of hell is a spiritual thief who will steal your right to heaven by teaching damnable heresies and doctrines of demons. Beware!

The Holy Spirit says of Jesus, "But this man, because He continueth ever, hath an unchangeable priesthood. Wherefore He is able also to save them to the uttermost that come unto God by Him, seeing He ever liveth to make intercession for them" (Heb. 7:24–25). Again, "Seeing then that we have a great high priest, that is passed into the heavens, JESUS THE SON OF GOD, let us hold fast our profession. For we have not an high priest (like some of the modern day religious confessors and mediators) which cannot be touched with our infirmities; but was in all points tempted like as we are, YET WITHOUT SIN. Let us therefore come boldly unto the throne of grace (please note: let us come boldly *to the throne of grace*—not to the pastor's study, not to the confessional, not to man or woman—but *to the throne of grace*), that we may obtain mercy, and find grace to help in time of need" (Heb. 4:14–16).

THE CHURCH (THE BUILDING OF GOD) IS INHABITED BY GOD THROUGH THE SPIRIT

Verses 19–22: "Now therefore ye are no more strangers, and foreigners, but fellowcitizens with the saints, and of the household of God; and are built upon the foundation of the apostles and prophets, Jesus Christ Himself being the chief corner stone; In whom all the building fitly framed together groweth unto an holy temple in the Lord: In whom ye also are builded together for an habitation of God through the Spirit."

Let me point out two words in these verses. They are found twice . . . the words, "IN WHOM." If there is any one thing clearly taught in Ephesians it is that all spiritual blessings are *in Christ*.

In chapter one, we are believers. At the close of chapter one we have the introduction to chapter two: "And hath put all things under His feet, and gave Him to be the head over all things to the church, which is His BODY, the fulness of Him that filleth all in all" (Eph. 1:22–23). Thus, in chapter two, believers are members of the one body . . . the body of Christ, and we become a member of that body through the baptism of the Holy Spirit (I Cor. 12:12). Chapter two closes by introducing chapter three: "In whom ye also are builded together for an habitation of God through the Spirit" (Eph. 2:22). We see first the believers, the next step we are members of His body; then we are the building inhabited by God through the Spirit.

Verse 19 opens with the words, "Now therefore . . . ." We were strangers——aliens, enemies; but now we are no longer strangers . . . we are believers, members of His body, fellow-citizens with all saints. We belong to the household of God, we are building upon the one Foundation, Jesus Christ (I Cor. 3:11). He is the chief cornerstone and in Him all the building——every believer, regardless of race——is framed together and is continually growing into the perfect body——the holy temple of the Lord. In Jesus we are builded together, and God inhabits the building through the Spirit. Beloved, it is too wonderful to take in, that we are the tabernacle of God . . . God lives in us! (II Peter 1:4). The divine nature abides in our bosom. We possess the Third Person of the Godhead . . . the Holy Spirit; therefore we should be very careful how we treat the temple in which God dwells.

We who were outcasts spiritually are now God's

household. We belong to the Father's family. We are the center of His love. We are also the Lord's temple . . . we are building upon the Chief Cornerstone; but that is not all: We are the habitation of the Spirit . . . He abides and lives in us.

When Jesus had by Himself purged our sins, when He had returned to the Father's side with the blood of Calvary, He then sent the Holy Spirit into the world, as promised to the disciples. And now, the Spirit abides within every believer. We are the habitation of God through the Spirit.

As I prepare these messages, I read in the daily papers where certain outstanding religious leaders are making pilgrimages to famous shrines . . . sacred spots, temples, cathedrals, etc. But let me remind you that the most sacred, the most holy, the most precious spot on this earth, so far as God is concerned, is not some shrine or temple, nor some church building. The spot that is supremely sacred to God is the place that God Himself has chosen as His habitation, His worshiping temple: *I am speaking of the heart of a born again believer.* In the words of Paul . . . "Yet not I, but Christ liveth in me" (Gal. 2:20). If that fact does not humble your heart, then my precious brother or sister in the Lord, I confess I know no Bible truth that would melt you within! To think that God would inhabit my heart certainly humbles me and melts my heart. God help me to keep the temple (this body) clean.

EPHESIANS — CHAPTER THREE

1. For this cause I Paul, the prisoner of Jesus Christ for you Gentiles,

2. If ye have heard of the dispensation of the grace of God which is given me to you-ward:

3. How that by revelation he made known unto me the mystery; (as I wrote afore in few words,

4. Whereby, when ye read, ye may understand my knowledge in the mystery of Christ)

5. Which in other ages was not made known unto the sons of men, as it is now revealed unto his holy apostles and prophets by the Spirit;

6. That the Gentiles should be fellowheirs, and of the same body, and partakers of his promise in Christ by the gospel:

7. Whereof I was made a minister, according to the gift of the grace of God given unto me by the effectual working of his power.

8. Unto me, who am less than the least of all saints, is this grace given, that I should preach among the Gentiles the unsearchable riches of Christ;

9. And to make all men see what is the fellowship of the mystery, which from the beginning of the world hath been hid in God, who created all things by Jesus Christ:

10. To the intent that now unto the principalities and powers in heavenly places might be known by the church the manifold wisdom of God,

11. According to the eternal purpose which he purposed in Christ Jesus our Lord:

12. In whom we have boldness and access with confidence by the faith of him.

13. Wherefore I desire that ye faint not at my tribulations for you, which is your glory.

14. For this cause I bow my knees unto the Father of our Lord Jesus Christ,

15. Of whom the whole family in heaven and earth is named,

16. That he would grant you, according to the riches of his glory, to be strengthened with might by his Spirit in the inner man;

17. That Christ may dwell in your hearts by faith; that ye, being rooted and grounded in love,

18. May be able to comprehend with all saints what is the breadth, and length, and depth, and height;

19. And to know the love of Christ, which passeth knowledge, that ye might be filled with all the fulness of God.

20. Now unto him that is able to do exceeding abundantly above all that we ask or think, according to the power that worketh in us,

21. Unto him be glory in the church by Christ Jesus throughout all ages, world without end. Amen.

THE MYSTERY OF THE CHURCH IS REVEALED

In the present chapter we will no longer be thinking in terms of the *Body*. We will think now in terms of the *Building* (Eph. 2:19–22), the mystical body of Christ which is the New Testament Church, formed through the power of His blood and the operation of the Holy Spirit. He who "borns" us and baptizes us into the body, produces or brings about the new man which God now has upon the earth. This new man (Eph. 2:15), is not the individual believer, but the *church*, considered as the body of Christ in the sense of Eph. 1:22–23, I Cor. 12:12–13, Col. 3:10–11, and of Heb. 12:23–24, which says, "To the general assembly and church of the firstborn, which are written in heaven, and to God the Judge of all, and to the spirits of just men made perfect, and to Jesus the mediator of the new covenant, and to the blood of sprinkling, that speaketh better things than that of Abel." This new man, brought about through the power of the blood, is made up of *Jews and Gentiles*, rich and poor, bond and free, by and through one principle only: *Faith in the finished work of the Lord Jesus*. Therefore those of us who are gathered together in this new organism . . . the new man, the new personality . . . henceforth constitute the people of God. We born again believers are fellow-citizens of God's commonwealth. Each and every believer is a child of God *individually*——and together, we make up the household of God.

In chapter two, we have our *position in Christ*: "YE IN ME." In chapter three, it is *possession of Christ*: "I IN YOU." We see this truth set forth in John, chapter 15:

"I am the vine, ye are the branches: He that abideth in me, and I in Him, the same bringeth forth much fruit: for without me ye can do nothing" (John 15:5). Jesus is the vine; we believers are the branches. In the vine we bring forth fruit——but apart from the vine we cannot produce fruit——and please notice that the vine *without the branches* does not produce fruit. It is the branches that bring forth fruit——but in order to bring forth fruit the branches must be connected to the vine: "Ye in Me—— and I in you."

In this glorious age of grace, believers (the new man) have access to Him. Jesus delights to have us come into His presence . . . yes, *boldly*——to make our requests known, and to allow Him to share our sorrows and our joys. As the new building, He has access to us . . . He abides in us. We are the temple of God.

Verses 1–8: "For this cause I Paul, the prisoner of Jesus Christ for you Gentiles, if ye have heard of the dispensation of the grace of God which is given me to you-ward: How that by revelation He made known unto me the mystery; (as I wrote afore in few words, whereby, when ye read, ye may understand my knowledge in the mystery of Christ) which in other ages was not made known unto the sons of men, as it is now revealed unto His holy apostles and prophets by the Spirit; That the Gentiles should be fellowheirs, and of the same body, and partakers of His promise in Christ by the Gospel: Whereof I was made a minister, according to the gift of the grace of God given unto me by the effectual working of His power. Unto me, who am less than the least of all saints, is this grace given, that I should preach among the Gentiles the unsearchable riches of Christ."

Throughout the third chapter, Paul is looking upon himself as the Holy-Spirit-appointed minister of the new covenant, the building of God. What Paul is saying is simply this: "You Gentile believers at Ephesus know well that I received this ministry on your behalf . . . the ministry with the message of God's marvelous grace, that

111

makes Gentiles fully equal with all others in the body of Christ. Because of this ministry——the Gospel that I have proclaimed without fear or favor——I am in prison. But I do not want you to faint or feel badly because of my bonds. Rather, I crown my labors on your behalf by turning to prayer, praying in the Spirit, presenting your need to the Heavenly Father, and beseeching the Father of our Lord Jesus Christ to 'grant you, according to the riches of His glory, to be strengthened with might by His Spirit in the inner man; that Christ may dwell in your hearts by faith; that ye, being rooted and grounded in love, may be able to comprehend and understand the great breadth, and length, and depth, and height; and to know the love of Christ, which passeth all understanding, that ye may be filled with all the fulness of God.' I am praying for you believers at Ephesus that you will go on, grow in grace and become full-grown believers, living examples of the grace of God."

In verse 3 Paul again points out that the Gospel he preached was by revelation, that he did not receive it by man nor from man, and that he did not consult the religious leaders at Jerusalem; but his message was direct from God by revelation. The message was the revelation of the mystery of Christ, which in other ages had not been made known unto the sons of men——but now God had been pleased to reveal unto His holy apostles and prophets (by the Holy Ghost) this great mystery, that the Gentiles should be fellowheirs and of the same body, there being no difference between Jew and Gentile.

In verse seven Paul states that he was made a minister according to the gift of grace. He did not take up the ministry as a vocation. He did not begin to preach the Gospel because his friends told him that he appeared to have the qualifications to make a good preacher. To-day some young men go to theological schools because their loved ones tell them they would make "a good preacher." Some young men go to theological institutions to learn how to preach. God have mercy on this poor ignorant age in which we live! God's ministers are *called* of God, *ordained* of God, *commissioned* of God, *sent by God* —and their message is *from* God. Paul was God's minister.

In verse two Paul refers to the "dispensation" of the grace of God, which God had given to him to reveal to the Gentiles. The word *dispensation* is a very interesting word. The Greek word is the word that is translated "house" in the English. Its full meaning is, "the law of the house." It means the regulation, or the management, of the house. The word can also be translated into English as "economy." So . . . during the Dispensation of Grace (the economy of grace) Paul was appointed by God the steward of this new law of the house, so to speak, or the one who would regulate the new management.

The same truth is clearly stated in Romans 11:13: "For I speak to you Gentiles, inasmuch as I am the apostle of the Gentiles, I magnify mine office." God appointed Paul a minister to the Gentiles in his experience on the Damascus road. Acts 9 gives the interesting story of Paul's conversion. He saw the Lord, he was stricken to the ground, the brightness of the face of Jesus blinded his eyes and he cried out, "Who art thou?" The voice from the sky answered, "I am Jesus whom thou persecutest." Then Paul said, "What wilt thou have me do?" And Jesus told him. From that point on, Jesus led and Saul of Tarsus followed. He thereby became Paul the preacher, the minister to the Gentiles. Paul's experience is a beautiful picture of what will happen when the nation Israel accepts the Lord. They will one day see Jesus. They will see the scars in His hands. They will ask Him where He received those scars and He will tell them,

"In the house of my friends." And a nation shall be saved in a day. Paul was born out of due season . . . He was saved when he saw the face of Jesus looking down from the sky as he traveled the Damascus road.

Suppose we look at the record: "But the Lord said unto him (Ananias), Go thy way: for he is a chosen vessel unto me, to bear my name before the Gentiles, and kings, and the children of Israel: For I will shew him how great things he must suffer for my name's sake" (Acts 9:15—16).

"But when it pleased God, who separated me from my mother's womb, AND CALLED ME BY HIS GRACE, to reveal His Son in me, that I might preach Him among the heathen (Gentiles); IMMEDIATELY I CONFERRED NOT WITH FLESH AND BLOOD" (Gal. 1:15—16).

"At midday, O king, I saw in the way a light from heaven, above the brightness of the sun (that light was none other than the brightness of the face of Jesus), shining round about me and them which journeyed with me. And when we were all fallen to the earth, I heard a voice speaking unto me, and saying in the Hebrew tongue, Saul, Saul, why persecutest thou me? It is hard for thee to kick against the pricks. And I said, Who art thou, Lord? And He said, I am Jesus whom thou persecutest. But rise, and stand upon thy feet: for I have appeared unto thee for this purpose, TO MAKE THEE A MINISTER AND A WITNESS BOTH OF THESE THINGS WHICH THOU HAST SEEN, AND OF THOSE THINGS IN THE WHICH I WILL APPEAR UNTO THEE; delivering thee from the people, and from the Gentiles, UNTO WHOM NOW I SEND THEE; to open their eyes, and to turn them from darkness to light, and from the power of Satan unto God, that they may receive forgiveness of sins, and inheritance among them which are sanctified by faith that is in Me" (Acts

114

26:13–18).

Therefore, I say that God gave to Paul the message, the doctrine, the rules and regulations for the management of the new building . . . the New Testament church. You will find the heart of the doctrine for the church in the Epistles, written through the inspiration of the Holy Spirit as Paul penned down these letters.

The word "mystery" used three times in these verses does not mean something mysterious, something that cannot be understood; but rather it means something that is made known only by revelation . . . something hidden until the proper and appointed time for that specific thing to be revealed or uncovered. I think this statement will substantiate what I said: "Which in other ages was not made known . . . as it is now revealed . . ." (Eph. 3:5). There are many mysteries referred to in the Word of God. Let me point out just a few here:

The mystery of the church——the Bride of Christ (Eph. 5:32).

The mystery of Christ indwelling us (Col. 1:27).

The mystery of the church——His body (Eph. 5 and our present chapter).

The mystery of Christ incarnate (I Tim. 3:16).

All of these mysteries were hidden in previous ages but are revealed in the New Testament. The mystery referred to in our present passage is "that the Gentiles should be fellowheirs, and of the same body, and partakers of His promise in Christ by the Gospel." It is only in the writings of the Apostle Paul that we find the position, the doctrine, the walk and the eternal destiny of the New Testament church, the body of Christ. The mystery "hid in God" was the divine purpose from the very beginning, to make Jews and Gentiles a wholly and entirely new thing . . . in reality a new organism (the church) which is the body of Christ, formed by and through the baptism with the Holy Ghost, and in which the distinction of Jew and Gentile disappears. This mystery is mentioned (but not explained) by Jesus when Peter said, "Thou art the Christ, the Son of the living God." Jesus said to Peter, "Blessed art thou, Simon Bar-jona: *for flesh and blood hath not revealed it unto thee*, BUT MY FATHER WHICH IS IN HEAVEN." Peter's testimony was not the product of human reasoning, nor of human ability. Jesus said, "Thou art Peter, and upon this rock (upon the testimony Peter had just given, a testimony that came by *revelation*, that Jesus was the virgin-born Son of God, yea, very God in flesh) I will build my church, and the gates of hell shall not prevail against it!" (Matt. 16:13ff).

The great mysteries of God can be known by man only by revelation directly from God. In Matthew Jesus states the mystery——but later He ordained Paul to receive the revelation of that mystery. That is what Paul is declaring in the third chapter of Ephesians.

It was extremely difficult for the Jew, during the transition period, to accept the fact that the Gentile "dogs" had become sons of God, co-heirs of God, co-members of the body of Christ, and co-sharers in the promise of the Spirit. The Jews just could not take it in. Read carefully Acts 15 . . . the entire chapter . . . and you will see that the Jews could not believe that Gentiles had received the blessings that had in former years been bestowed only upon God's chosen nation, Israel.

Many times we hear ministers crying long and loud, "To the Jew first . . . to the Jew first . . . to the Jew first!" Yes——I love the Jew, I want the Jew saved, I believe in Jewish missions; but my precious friend, the Jew *had* his chance first! God offered Jesus to the Jew.

Pilate said, "I have Jesus and Barabbas; whom shall I release? Whom do you want?" And they said, "Give us Barabbas! Kill Jesus! Let His blood be upon us and upon our children!" God called Paul to make known "the mystery" unto a people who were not a people. Because Israel refused to accept the kingdom, God turned to a people less favored by Him, and through that people now flow the blessings of God's grace to all who will hear and believe the good news of the Gospel.

The revelation of the church, and the good news of the Gospel of the grace of God was committed unto Paul. In his own words he said, "Whereof I was made a minister, according to the gift of the grace of God given unto me by the effectual working of His power."

In Galatians 1:12 Paul says, "For I neither received it (the ministry, the message) of man, neither was I taught it (by teachers in the flesh), BUT BY THE REVELATION OF JESUS CHRIST."

Paul unmistakeably traces his message back to divine origin. The message concerning the "gift of grace" came to Paul by and through "the working of power" . . . the power of the Holy Ghost. The exalted position of the Apostle Paul, the heavenly revelation that came to him, did not puff him up——or as we would say, "It did not give him the big-head." But instead, it humbled his heart: "Unto me WHO AM LESS THAN THE LEAST OF ALL SAINTS is this grace given." Those words could come only from a heart totally and entirely possessed by the Holy Ghost and surrendered to the will of God. I do not believe any man who ever lived on this earth was ever more completely surrendered to God's sovereign will than was the Apostle Paul.

Writing to the young preacher, Timothy, Paul declared that he (Paul) was chiefest of sinners (I Tim. 1:15b).

117

Writing to the believers in Corinth, he said concerning himself that he was the least of the apostles, not meet (worthy) to be called an apostle (I Cor. 15:9). And in our present chapter he makes known his humble spirit by saying, "I am less than the least of all saints" (verse 8). It seems to me that Paul is endeavoring to get across to the Ephesians (and to us) this fact:

"Just think of it! Can you imagine . . . to my trust God has committed the Gospel! I am chief of sinners . . . I wasted the church . . . I persecuted the followers of Jesus. Yet God has counted me faithful, putting me in the ministry and revealing to me the mystery of the body of Christ . . . the New Testament Church!"

Paul was faithful to his call and to his commission. Just before he was beheaded for his testimony, as he looked death in the face, he looked up to heaven and said, "The time of my departure is at hand. I have fought a good fight. I have finished my course. I have kept the faith. There is therefore laid up for me a crown of life!"

In Ephesians 3:8 Paul also seems to be saying, "And to think that I, a Jew, am called and commissioned to take this good news to the Gentiles . . . to make known unto them the unsearchable riches of Christ!"

Any part of Christ can be summed up in one word: UNSEARCHABLE! When we attempt to describe "the unsearchable riches of Christ" words fail us; but I am sure that Paul must have had in mind the fact that Jesus was in the beginning with the Father, in the bosom of the Father, the most precious jewel in heaven, co-equal with God the Father, Creator of all things. Nothing was made without Him, but by Him all things were made. He was worshiped and honored in heaven because He was Deity, co-equal with the Father. Paul thought of the riches of Christ's willingness to leave all of heaven's

118

glory, honor, and praise, and come into the world to lay His life down in the most shameful, cursed way that any man could die; and I think Paul has the riches of His grace in mind when he says to the believers in Corinth, ". . . though He (Jesus) was rich, yet for your sakes He became poor, that ye through His poverty might become rich" (II Cor. 8:9). To the Philippians Paul said that even though Jesus was equal with God, He took a body of humiliation, became obedient unto death . . . even the death of the cross. I am sure Paul was thinking of the riches of the sinless life of Jesus here on earth. No man ever lived like Jesus lived. No man ever spoke like Jesus spoke. No man ever worked miracles like Jesus did. No man ever loved like Jesus loved. Everything He did was so different to the way other men would have done it (if they could have done it)! When Jesus performed His wonders, the people said, "We never saw it on this wise."

Then—Paul must have thought of the exceeding riches Jesus demonstrated, in that He never one time complained or grumbled. He said, "Foxes have holes, the birds have nests—but the Son of man has nowhere to lay His head!" He borrowed a boat for a pulpit. Many nights He spent alone, in the Garden in prayer. He had no lunch —but He took a little boy's lunch and fed five thousand. He never performed a miracle of any kind to bring comfort or profit to Himself. Surely Paul must have been thinking of the exceeding riches of His sacrifice, His unselfishness, His kindness, His goodness, His generosity—and then of course the riches of His death:

He came—and announced clearly that He was in the world—not to be ministered unto, but to minister and to give His life a ransom for many. He did just that. When men reviled Him He did not scold them—He said, "Father, forgive them! They do not know what they are doing!"

When men called Him ugly names He did not fight back. At the beginning, both thieves railed on Him, mocked Him, sneered and jeered even though they were in the same condemnation. Finally, one of the thieves saw something in Jesus, or heard something fall from His lips, that changed his mind, and he cried out, "Lord, remember me when thou comest into thy kingdom." Jesus in His dying hour saved a thief who had been His enemy but moments earlier. Any phase of the life, ministry, death, burial and resurrection of Jesus can be described as "unsearchable."

My precious friend, you may be poor in this world, so far as goods and the secular things of life are concerned. Your belongings and your wealth may be very meager—— but you can be a multi-millionaire in the grace of God! Through His poverty, you can be as rich as heaven's unsearchable riches.

FOR WHOM
ARE THE UNSEARCHABLE RICHES OF CHRIST?

Verses 9—12: "And to make all men see what is the fellowship of the mystery, which from the beginning of the world hath been hid in God, who created all things by Jesus Christ: To the intent that now unto the principalities and powers in heavenly places might be known by the church the manifold wisdom of God, according to the eternal purpose which He purposed in Christ Jesus our Lord: *In whom* (in Jesus) we have boldness and confidence by the faith of Him."

God had given to Paul the message that was directed to all. Regardless of class or nationality, the Gospel of the grace of God is open to all . . . there is no select, elect, chosen group in this marvelous day of grace. The *body of Christ* was elected before the foundation of the world; but *you*, my dear friend, as an individual, must accept Jesus Christ as your personal Saviour.

Think of it! The message that was "hid in God" had been entrusted to a Gospel preacher, and it astonished Paul, humbled his heart, to think that he, "the chief of sinners," was the one to whom God had entrusted the glorious message of Grace that had been hid in God from eternity——yea, from the beginning.

I say this humbly——not sarcastically——but if some of the scientists, chemists and astrologers who are attempting to probe outer space to discover how this earth was formed, could talk with Paul for a few moments, he could clear up the whole question for them. Paul did not have the telescopes nor the rockets that modern chemists, scientists and astrologers have . . . but Paul knew God. And God Almighty revealed to him that all things were made "by Jesus Christ." Paul knew the God who created all things by Jesus Christ, and he preached that God to all and sundry.

We are living in the age of skepticism and infidelity. Those of us who embrace the Word of God have no doubt as to how creation came about. In Genesis chapter one, the name "God" occurs thirty-one times——and certainly stands to defend the truth that God is the Creator of the universe. He is responsible for the orderly arrangement of the planets and constellations which have been speeding through outer space for ages upon ages . . . without catastrophe! Only God Almighty could create this universe and all that goes with it! In my Scofield Bible I have underlined Genesis 1:1 . . . the first four words: "In the beginning——GOD . . . ." And I have written in the margin, "I have no trouble believing all the rest." Think it over: If God is God, then certainly I have no trouble believing that God could do exceeding abundantly

121

above anything that I can ever conceive.

Verse 10 mentions principalities and powers in heavenly places. In the heavenlies just above us, there are principalities and powers . . . rulers of spiritual wickedness in high places. In Ephesians 6:12–17 we have Scriptures that enlighten us concerning these principalities, powers, and rulers of darkness.

Beyond the heaven just above us we have *good* principalities and powers . . . cherubims, seraphims, the archangels, the angels of God. God Himself is there, with the Son and all the saints. But in our present Scripture Paul is serving notice on principalities and powers that the church has the message that will eventually write "Finished" across Satan and his kingdom. (When I say *church*, I am not talking about the brick building with a steeple on it . . . I am speaking of the body of Christ, made up of born again, blood-washed, redeemed sons of God.) The devil knows that his days are numbered. He is a defeated foe——and he knows it! That is the reason he labors untiringly and without ceasing in an effort to damn every soul he can. Satan desires to delay the coming of Jesus for His church as long as he can possibly delay it, because Satan knows that when the Rapture takes place, his days are few. The events that follow the Rapture lead to the devil's being placed in the bottomless pit forever. Satan knows that. There are many Christians who are ignorant concerning the events that lie ahead, but Satan is not ignorant. He is "transformed as an angel of light." Before he became the devil, he was "perfect in wisdom."

In verse 11 Paul makes known that all of this will happen according to the eternal purpose of Christ Jesus, our Lord. Earlier in this series I gave you Scriptures from Acts 15 showing that God has a blueprint, and known

122

unto God are all His works and ways from the beginning. Before God ever made this earth or a planet or a constellation, He completed His program throughout eternity until eternity. Everything is working according to the plan and program of Almighty God.

As I prepare this message, I read in the papers and leading periodicals concerning the gigantic ecumenical council of churches and religious leaders of earth. I read of the rockets, and the probes into outer space. I read concerning man's braggadocio declaration that he will go to the moon, and use the moon as a springboard to reach Mars! And then I remember that every major judgment God has sent upon this earth was preceded by the desire of God's creatures to by-pass God and become gods themselves. Daniel was reminded that in the end KNOWLEDGE WOULD INCREASE, and men would be on the move, running to and fro. Beloved, prophetically speaking, we are living in the last hours of this day of Grace.

In verse 12, we have those two familiar words, "in whom" . . . that is, *in Jesus* . . . we have boldness, "and access with confidence by the faith of Him." That is a tremendous verse. It does not seem like much, just to read it hurriedly; but it is tremendous. IN JESUS we approach God boldly. If you will permit me to use an expression from the farm (I was reared on a farm, and I thank God for it), we often referred to a dog that would kill sheep and calves, as a "sheep-killing dog." Oftentimes that term was used in connection with a despicable person who had committed a crime. God does not want us to approach Him in the manner of a sheep-killing dog. We were Gentile dogs——aliens, strangers, hateful, ungodly; but NOW we are righteous in Christ, sons of God; and therefore, because we ARE sons through the redemption in Jesus' blood, we are invited to approach God the Father boldly, in Jesus——not in our name or in our power, but in His name. When we approach God in Jesus we have access into the very presence of God Almighty . . . and we have access with confidence. We do not fear or doubt, because we have faith in Jesus and He is very able to perform everything He promised, everything He does promise His child.

Paul had a message to deliver to all peoples, and he faithfully delivered that message until he sealed his ministry and his testimony with his life's blood.

PAUL'S PRAYER FOR THE EPHESIANS
THAT THEY MAY EXPERIENCE
THE FULNESS OF THE SPIRIT AND KNOWLEDGE

Verses 13—21: "Wherefore I desire that ye faint not at my tribulation for you, which is your glory. For this cause I bow my knees unto the Father of our Lord Jesus Christ, of whom the whole family in heaven and earth is named, that He would grant you, according to the riches of His glory, to be strengthened with might by His Spirit in the inner man; that Christ may dwell in your hearts by faith; that ye, being rooted and grounded in love, may be able to comprehend with all saints what is the breadth, and length, and depth, and height; and to know the love of Christ, which passeth knowledge, that ye might be filled with all the fulness of God. Now unto Him that is able to do exceeding abundantly above all that we ask or think, according to the power that worketh in us, unto Him be glory in the church by Christ Jesus throughout all ages, world without end. Amen."

In Ephesians 1:15—18, Paul prayed that God would give to the Ephesians the spirit of wisdom and revelation *in knowledge*, that the eyes of their understanding might be enlightened, that they might know the hope of His calling and the riches of His glory; but here in chapter three,

Paul is praying that the believers at Ephesus will be *strengthened in the inner man*, and that they will know the love of God, that they will be rooted and grounded in the love of God.

It makes no difference how much knowledge or wisdom we may have concerning the things of God, if we do not demonstrate love we are worthless to the cause of Christ. To the Corinthians, Paul expressed it in these words:

"Though I speak with the tongues of men and of angels, and have not love, I am become as sounding brass, or a tinkling cymbal. And though I have the gift of prophecy, and understand all mysteries, and all knowledge; and though I have all faith, so that I could remove mountains, and have not love, I am nothing. And though I bestow all my goods to feed the poor, and though I give my body to be burned, and have not love, it profiteth me nothing" (I Cor. 13:1-3).

Regardless of what we are and what we do, if we do not possess the love of God, and if what we do is not permeated by the love of God, then spiritually speaking we are just one big nothing!

There is an interesting truth set forth in verse 14, about which we hear very little today. Most of us overlook it. Paul said, "I BOW MY KNEES." I am not judging, nor am I being sarcastic; but not many Christians bend their knees when they pray. Some do, but today most praying is done in standing or sitting position. There was a time when God's minister bowed upon his knees in the pulpit . . . thank God, many still do; but there was a time when ALL preachers bowed upon their knees to talk to the Heavenly Father. I realize there is no glory in the position of the body while praying . . . it is the condition of the heart that counts; but to me, bowing upon one's knees denotes humility . . . and we do know that God gives

125

grace to the humble while He resists the proud.

Notice the order of prayer: Paul bowed to the Heavenly Father. He prayed in the name of Christ the Son (verse 17). He prayed that the Christians might be strengthened through——or by——the Holy Spirit in the inner man.

To the believers at Rome Paul said, "Likewise the Spirit also helpeth our infirmities: for we know not what we should pray for as we ought: but the Spirit itself maketh intercession for us with groanings which cannot be uttered. And He that searcheth the hearts knoweth what is the mind of the Spirit, because He maketh intercession for the saints according to the will of God" (Rom. 8:26–27). If we hope for God to hear our prayers, we must pray in the Spirit, because God honors no prayer that is not in the Spirit. The Spirit searches the hearts of believers, and the Spirit knows the will of God. God honors the prayer prayed *in the Spirit* because that prayer is prayed according to the will of God. In this day of grace, we *bow in reverence to the Heavenly Father*, we make our requests *in the name of Jesus the Son*, and we *depend upon the Holy Spirit* to bring results in prayer——because He (the Spirit) makes intercession to God through our one Mediator, the Lord Jesus Christ (I Tim. 2:5, I John 2:1–2).

Jesus said, "And I will pray the Father, and He shall give you another Comforter, that He may abide with you for ever" (John 14:16). Again, "If any man love me, he will keep my words: and my Father will love him, and we will come unto him, and make our abode with him" (John 14:23). Again, "If ye abide in me, and my words abide in you, ye shall ask what ye will, and it shall be done . . ." (John 15:7). That promise is to believers who are fully consecrated, spiritually minded, and through the knowledge of the Word they pray in the Spirit. Such a prayer is answered because it is prayed according to the will of God.

Notice in verse 15, the whole family in heaven and in earth bears the namesake of Christ. Of course, the name "Christian" is "Christ" softened by adding "-ian." The disciples were called Christians first at Antioch:

". . . And it came to pass, that a whole year they assembled themselves with the church, and taught much people. And the disciples were called Christians first at Antioch" (Acts 11:26).

(The preceding verses in Acts 11 show us that Paul was one of the first to be called Christian.)

Please notice——the family of God is now separated. By that, I mean some believers are in Paradise, resting, while others are on earth, walking and laboring. But the family in heaven and on earth is ONE FAMILY, and bears the namesake of our Saviour, the Lord Jesus Christ.

In verse 16, Paul is not praying that the believers at Ephesus might *receive* the Spirit——they already possess the Spirit. He is praying that God, through Christ and the riches of His glory, will strengthen the believers by the Spirit, "in the inner man." All born again believers possess the Holy Spirit (Gal. 4:6, I Cor. 12:13, Rom. 8:9, Rom. 8:14, Rom. 8:16, Eph. 4:32, John 3:5). There is no such thing as salvation apart from the possession of the Holy Spirit. I say this in love and tenderness——but there is much ignorance among believers concerning the ministry of the Holy Spirit in this Dispensation of Grace. The Holy Ghost came on the day of Pentecost. The church was born . . . one hundred and twenty members were baptized into that body; and since that day the Holy Ghost takes up His abode in the heart of every believer the split second that believer exercises faith in the finished work of Jesus. We will learn later in this Epistle that not all believers are *filled* with the Holy Spirit. One can possess the Holy Spirit and yet not be filled with or by the Spirit. We will study this more fully when we reach that particular chapter.

Notice—Paul prays for strength in THE INNER MAN. There are those who close their eyes to the Bible truth of the two natures*. Paul was not praying that they would be strengthened in the flesh. I know God does strengthen believers in the flesh—and we need to be strengthened in our body; but we need strength in the inner man. Nicodemus was a sincere seeker of truth. He came to Jesus in the right spirit, and Jesus told him, "Except a man be born of the Spirit . . . he cannot enter the kingdom of God." He further enlightened Nicodemus by explaining, "That which is born of the flesh is flesh, and that which is born of the Spirit is spirit" (John 3:6).

When a sinner is saved, the flesh is not born again. The inner man, the spirit, is born of the Spirit. Believers walk differently, talk differently, live differently, because there is a new creation in the heart from which proceed the issues of life. And my dear reader, until you know the truth concerning the two natures—the flesh and the spirit—you will never enjoy your spiritual birthright, which is "life abundantly."

Paul prayed that the blessing would be granted "according to His riches in glory." In Philippians, Paul uses that term to assure the believers at Philippi (and to assure US) that out of God's inexhaustible supply, He is very capable and willing to supply all our need.

In verse 17 Paul is not praying that Christ may come into the hearts of the Ephesians, but that by faith Christ

*For further study concerning the two natures of a believer, order my book "The Two Natures." Order from The Gospel Hour, Inc., Box 2024, Greenville, S. C.

may *dwell* in their hearts . . . that is, that He will abide in or completely control and permeate the heart. This truth is drastically needed by some believers today. John said, "And now . . . abide in Him; that when He shall appear, we may have confidence, and not be ashamed before Him at His coming" (I John 2:28).

Some believers will be ashamed when they stand before God. This is clearly taught in the Word of God. Salvation is of the Lord . . . totally and entirely of the Lord; but rewards are earned according to our faithful stewardship——not how much we do, but faithfulness is what counts in rewards. Paul wanted the believers at Ephesus to be wholeheartedly surrendered. He wanted Christ to abide every second of every moment, and control every minute detail of the heart. He said, "Whether you eat or drink, or whatsoever you do, do it all to the glory of God." One must be an abiding, believing, trusting, fully-committed believer to practice such spiritual living moment by moment.

Notice that Christ may dwell in your hearts "BY FAITH." There are many who depend upon their feelings . . . and if they do not feel like they think a Christian should feel, they think they are not saved, or that they are backslidden, or that they are not what they should be for Jesus. But it is not by feelings . . . it is "by faith." Faith rests upon God's Word because the Word is God and God cannot lie (Heb. 6:18, Titus 1:2).

The only way for a believer to abide in Christ, the only way to be continually conscious of the abiding presence of Jesus——not just in church or in a prayer meeting, but every second of every day, *is by faith.* "Faith cometh by hearing, and hearing by the Word of God" (Rom. 10:17). Therefore we must be a student of the Word. We must be a lover of the Word, we must "eat" the Word (John 6) if we hope to be what we ought to be, spiritually, and if we hope to enjoy our spiritual birthright.

Faith is the key that unlocks a wonderful, transforming experience in the life of believers when they will commit themselves to devoted Bible study . . . hear the Word and believe what the Word promises. You need not ever put a question mark around anything God has said in His precious Word.

In verses 18 and 19, Paul continues in prayer, requesting that the believers at Ephesus, along with *"all* saints" (that takes in you and me) may know and understand the breadth, the length, the depth and the height . . . and know the love of God which passeth knowledge, "that ye (believers) might be filled with ALL THE FULNESS OF GOD."

Just here, I would like to point out some things about the love of God that will enrich your life if you will study carefully the references I will give. It is impossible for me to give you the text here, but I will give you the references, and you study them in your Bible:

The origin of love is divine (I John 4:8).

Love has been from everlasting (Gen. 1:1, Psalm 90:1-2).

The source of pure love is God (II Cor. 13:11).

We love God because He first loved us (I John 4:17).

Love is the evidence of saving faith in Jesus (I John 4:19).

Love is the royal badge of true discipleship (John 13:35).

Love is the assurance that we have passed from death unto life (I John 3:14).

The love of God in our heart is unmerited (Col. 1: 12-14).

The love of God is the most costly thing known to heaven or earth (Eph. 1:7).

The love of God is free to all who will receive it (Rom. 3:24–25).

The love of God is universal in its offer (John 3:16).

The love of God is unbounded in its work (Eph. 2:4).

The love of God is unbroken in its ministry (Rom. 8:39).

The love of God is great (Eph. 2:4).

The love of God is inconceivable (Eph. 3:19).

The love of God is unselfish (I John 4:10).

The love of God is forever unchanging (John 13:1).

The love of God is inseparable (Rom. 8:35–39).

The love of God is everlasting (Jer. 31:3).

The love of God is perfect (I John 4:18).

Do not forget that all spiritual blessings are "in Christ," and to the believer Christ is better than the best, He is richer than the richest. The Holy Spirit describes Him thus:

The love of Christ is unknowable (Eph. 3:19).

The riches of Christ are unsearchable (Eph. 3:8).

The joy He gives is unspeakable (I Peter 1:8).

The ways of Christ are untrackable (Rom. 11:33).

The grace of the Lord Jesus is inexhaustible (II Cor. 9:8).

The peace of Christ is unfathomable (Phil. 4:7).

Jesus Christ Himself is unsurpassable (Ex. 15:11).

The Lord Jesus Christ is the mightiest among the holy. The Lord Jesus Christ is the holiest among the mighty. With His pierced hands He is able to lift empires out of the mire and the muck of lust and sin. He governs all ages, from the eternity behind us through the eternity

131

that lies ahead. I have already made the statement that if the ocean were a giant inkwell filled with ink, and if every stalk on earth were a quill, and every person on earth were a scribe as the beautiful song declares, it would still be impossible to write the love of God even though the sky were parchment and we had the vastness of the blue upon which to write! We could never describe the love of God. The love of God "passeth knowledge." It is humanly impossible for the finite mind to comprehend the love of God.

Its breadth—"God so loved the world." Can you conceive of such love? Do you dare ask yourself what it would mean to love the whole wide world? How many folks do you love? Think it over. The breadth of God's love covers the whole wide world.

Its length—"God gave His only begotten Son." God's love reached from the portals of glory to a stable in Bethlehem. God's love placed His only Son in the womb of the virgin Mary. He was born . . . He lived . . . God gave Him. God surrendered His Son into the hands of wicked sinners, and they nailed Him to a cross. That, in some small way, points out the length of the love of God. Do you have a son? Do you have an only child? Would you surrender your child to die for wicked men?

Its depth—"Whosoever believeth in Him should not perish." Oh, I know we say we love everybody . . . but do we? Do we really love everybody? It is easy to love the lovely. It is easy to love those who are always doing kind things for you and saying kind things about you— but God so loved that He gave His only Son, that whosoever . . . the lovely, the unlovely . . . might not perish. Christ died for the ungodly. God surrendered up Jesus when we were yet sinners.

Its height—"Everlasting life." The love of God

reaches to the depth of sin and places that sinner in the heavenlies in Christ Jesus. From the lowest depths to the highest height . . . only the love of God could work such a miracle!

BE FILLED WITH ALL THE FULNESS OF GOD. It is possible for a person to possess God and not be completely filled with (possess the fulness of) the spiritual blessings provided in Christ by the love of God.

God proposes to flood our life with His fulness, that, filled with Himself, there shall not be found room for the fretful, shameful things of self. God wants us to have a fulness of life that will displace self with Himself, a life that will keep the heart of His child centered on HIM.

Let me clearly state that you do not receive redemption in parts. Salvation is a Person . . . Jesus Christ . . . and we are totally born when we are saved. But it is possible to possess salvation and not be possessed by the Holy Spirit in the fullest sense. We are commanded to yield our bodies, the members of our bodies, into the hands of the Holy Spirit.

Verse 20 describes the limitless One who is able. Paul uses the term "able" many times when referring to Jesus in his letters to the believers.

Christ is able to do all that we ask or even think.

Christ is able to do *above* all that we ask or think.

Christ is able to do *abundantly* above all that we ask or think.

But that is not all! Christ is able to do EXCEEDING abundantly above all we ask or think!

Do you agree that here is displayed the limitless One? You name the need . . . God is able to supply that need in Christ, but *only* in Christ. We must pray in the Spirit, and when we pray in the Spirit we will not pray foolish prayers. Let me assure you that whatsoever you need as a believer in Christ, that need is already met; claim it! It is yours. He is able to do exceeding abundantly above all that we ask or think,——and the miracle happens according to the power "that worketh in us" . . . not around us, not on the outside——but WITHIN. Thank God, Christianity abides within. Man-made religion demands outward works and demonstrations. Poor religionists many times must make long journeys to worship; but thank God the One whom we worship is nearer than even our breath; *He abides in our heart.*

The last verse in our present chapter gives to God the glory by Christ the Son, in the church. Paul was jealous for Jesus. Paul wanted all honor and glory to be directed to the Lord Jesus Christ. He did not crave nor accept praise from men for himself. To God be the glory . . . He is worthy; and Paul said, "I count all things loss that I might gain Christ!" He wanted Jesus to have pre-eminence in everything . . . in the life of the individual, in the church, in every minute detail of daily living . . . eating, drinking, whatsoever we do——Paul declares we should "do it all to the glory of God." Today I wonder how Jesus feels, I wonder how the heart of God feels, when men are praised to high heaven, while Jesus seemingly takes a back seat?

"Now when Solomon had made an end of praying . . . the glory of the Lord filled the house. And the priests could not enter into the house of the Lord, because the glory of the Lord had filled the Lord's house" (II Chron. 7:1–2).

When the tabernacle was finished and everything was put in its proper place——"Then a cloud covered the tent of the congregation, and the glory of the Lord filled the tabernacle" (Exodus 40:34).

"Blessed be the Lord God of Israel from everlasting to everlasting: and let all the people say, Amen" (Psalm 106:48).

My fellow believer, do you not agree that our "able-abundantly-above-all" God is worthy of all honor, glory, praise, adoration and worship?

Some of the promises and some of the deep spiritual teachings of chapter three may cause you to wonder. You may stagger at the depth of such statements. You may ask, "How CAN these things be true? How can these things come about in my individual experience?" Let me answer by saying, "THE ABILITY OF GOD." If God is God, then do not stagger at His promises. His ability will handle any and all need brought to Him by any and all believers.

He is able to deliver in the hour of a peril that seems impossible to be delivered from—as in the case of Daniel (Daniel 3:17).

He is able to deliver from any and all temptation (I Cor. 10:13, Heb. 2:9).

He has the power and He is able to heal when all else fails (Matt. 9:28).

He is able to save the vilest, the most despicable. His love reaches down to the uttermost (Heb. 7:25).

He is able to quicken and make alive that which is dead (Eph. 2:1, Rom. 4:21).

After saving the soul, He is able to keep that soul from stumbling, staggering, or falling (Jude 24).

His grace is unknown—He is able to make ALL grace abound in the hour of the need for grace (II Cor. 9:8).

He is able to carry out, perform, supply every promise made anywhere in the Holy Bible, including the amazing promises in Ephesians (Eph. 3:20).

The only condition to be met to lay claim on the promises of God is to totally and entirely submit soul, spirit and body to God:

"And the very God of peace sanctify you wholly; and I pray God your whole spirit and soul and body be preserved blameless unto the coming of our Lord Jesus Christ" (I Thess. 5:23).

EPHESIANS — CHAPTER FOUR

1. I therefore, the prisoner of the Lord, beseech you that ye walk worthy of the vocation wherewith ye are called,

2. With all lowliness and meekness, with longsuffering, forbearing one another in love;

3. Endeavouring to keep the unity of the Spirit in the bond of peace.

4. There is one body, and one Spirit, even as ye are called in one hope of your calling;

5. One Lord, one faith, one baptism,

6. One God and Father of all, who is above all, and through all, and in you all.

7. But unto every one of us is given grace according to the measure of the gift of Christ.

8. Wherefore he saith, When he ascended up on high, he led captivity captive, and gave gifts unto men.

9. (Now that he ascended, what is it but that he also descended first into the lower parts of the earth?

10. He that descended is the same also that ascended up far above all heavens, that he might fill all things.)

11. And he gave some, apostles; and some, prophets; and some, evangelists; and some, pastors and teachers;

12. For the perfecting of the saints, for the work of the ministry, for the edifying of the body of Christ:

13. Till we all come in the unity of the faith, and of the knowledge of the Son of God, unto a perfect man, unto the measure of the stature of the fulness of Christ:

14. That we henceforth be no more children, tossed to and fro, and carried about with every wind of doctrine, by the sleight of men, and cunning craftiness, whereby they lie in wait to deceive;

15. But speaking the truth in love, may grow up into him in all things, which is the head, even Christ:

16. From whom the whole body fitly joined together and compacted by that which every joint supplieth, according to the effectual working in the measure of every part, maketh increase of the body unto the edifying of itself in love.

17. This I say therefore, and testify in the Lord, that ye henceforth walk not as other Gentiles walk, in the vanity of their mind,

18. Having the understanding darkened, being alienated from the life of God through the ignorance that is in them, because of the blindness of their heart:

19. Who being past feeling have given themselves over unto lasciviousness, to work all uncleanness with greediness.

20. But ye have not so learned Christ;

21. If so be that ye have heard him, and have been taught by him, as the truth is in Jesus:

22. That ye put off concerning the former conversation the old man,

which is corrupt according to the deceitful lusts;

23. And be renewed in the spirit of your mind;

24. And that ye put on the new man, which after God is created in righteousness and true holiness.

25. Wherefore putting away lying, speak every man truth with his neighbour: for we are members one of another.

26. Be ye angry, and sin not: let not the sun go down upon your wrath:

27. Neither give place to the devil.

28. Let him that stole steal no more: but rather let him labour, working with his hands the thing which is good, that he may have to give to him that needeth.

29. Let no corrupt communication proceed out of your mouth, but that which is good to the use of edifying, that it may minister grace unto the hearers.

30. And grieve not the holy Spirit of God, whereby ye are sealed unto the day of redemption.

31. Let all bitterness, and wrath, and anger, and clamour, and evil speaking, be put away from you, with all malice:

32. And be ye kind one to another, tenderhearted, forgiving one another, even as God for Christ's sake hath forgiven you.

THE WALK AND SERVICE OF A BELIEVER

In chapter one we studied the most wonderful story ever heard . . . the story of how God provided redemption in Christ.

In chapter two we learned that believers are a living organism . . . the church is made up of born again persons, members of the most wonderful body ever known.

In chapter three we learned further that we are the building of God . . . yea, we are the temple of the Holy Spirit. All believers are built together into one holy temple, the habitation of God.

In our present chapter, Paul begins to outline the walk and the service of the believer.

Verses 1–3: "I therefore, the prisoner of the Lord, beseech you that ye walk worthy of the vocation wherewith ye are called, with all lowliness and meekness, with longsuffering, forbearing one another in love; endeavouring to keep the unity of the Spirit in the bond of peace."

Notice Paul reminds them again that he is a prisoner of the Lord. He is not in prison for wrong doing . . . he is in prison for the sake of the Gospel.

The Christian walk and service are not according to man made rules or standards. It does not mean that we are supposed to sign a pledge that we will not go here or there, nor do this or that. We are to walk worthy of the name "Christian." In us Jesus must find His earthly walk. He lives in our bodies, He walks in our bodies —and we are the Bible the world reads. We present the only Christ the world will ever know. If the world does not see Jesus in us, then we are not walking worthy of the Christ who lives within us. In Bible language He ". . . dwells in us and walks in us" (II Cor. 6:16).

We believers are the body of Christ. We represent Him in this earth; by our actions we express to others what Christ is. They measure Christ by the way we walk. We prove to others by the way we walk that we have had a change of heart, and that we are a new creature. When the Israelites journeyed in the Old Testament era, the tabernacle (which was carried by the Levites) actually walked in their midst. In the same manner, Jesus says to us and of us, "Ye are the temple of the living God; as God hath said, I will dwell in them, and walk in them" (II Cor. 6:16).

In their daily walk, believers are to express both the *life* (of the body), and the presence of righteousness in our daily living. We are new creations in Christ—but we are more than that: We possess divine nature. We are to produce righteous living, a righteous walk. The fruit we bear outwardly testifies what we possess inwardly. As spiritually minded believers, we are to be imitators of Christ.

The gift of God——His only begotten Son——makes us one with Christ. We are born into the family of God, we become a member of the body of Christ. The graces produced in our life by the presence and the power of the Holy Spirit, manifest newness of life in our daily walk. Because we are sons of God, and because we are the temple of the Holy Spirit, we should bring glory and honor to God. We certainly should be an example of grace. We should be an epistle read of men.

It seems to me that Paul was saying to the believers at Ephesus, "I am a prisoner, I am in bonds for the Gospel's sake; but you believers are free. Your responsibility is greater than mine. You must not use your freedom to satisfy your own desires and pleasures, but you must walk worthy of the vocation wherewith you have been called."

Although Paul was sitting in a dungeon, his testimony to the guards was a true testimony; but the Ephesian believers had a much greater opportunity to witness than Paul had. You and I are read of men, whether you know it or not. They watch us, they listen to us when we talk. They check the places we go, the things we do, the company we keep, the songs we sing. As representatives of the Lord Jesus in a wicked world, we should be very careful as to what we do and how we walk.

In Paul's letters to the believers, he refers to our calling as the "high calling" (Phil. 3:14). Also a "holy calling" (II Tim. 1:9) and a "heavenly calling" (Heb. 3:1). We are to walk in a way that will be worthy of our high, holy, heavenly calling. We are to walk "with all lowliness and meekness." We are to walk with "long-suffering, forbearing one another in love, giving diligence to keep the unity of the Spirit in the bond of peace." To walk in this path of righteousness can be accomplished only by and through full surrender to the Holy Spirit.

We are to endeavor to keep the unity of the Spirit and the bond of peace. We are admonished, "Grieve not the Spirit," "quench not the Spirit," and "be filled with the Spirit." Believers should spend much time searching the Scriptures, and thereby learn the truth concerning the ministry of the Holy Spirit in and through us during this dispensation of the grace of God.

Verses 4—6: "There is one body, and one Spirit, even as ye are called in one hope of your calling; One Lord, one faith, one baptism, one God and Father of us all, who is above all, and through all, and in you all."

In connection with these verses, please read John chapter seventeen in its entirety. Study it carefully, and hear the cry of the Lord Jesus as He begs for oneness in the body——the church. Surely it must grieve the great heart of God and of the Lord Jesus Christ when He looks down upon His people and sees the existing division and strife among Christians.

The term "religious bigots" has come into prominence in recent months. The reason? Some spiritually minded ministers and Christians have dared take a stand against error. And because we cry long and earnestly that there is only one way to enter heaven's glory; because we declare that Christianity is the one——and only——religion that is right, many of us have been branded "bigots." We are informed by the enemies of the cross that every man has a right to his religion just as much as we have a right to what we believe; but I want to say emphatically, dogmatically, without apology and without hesitation that no man has any right to a religion other than that purchased by Jesus by the shedding of His own blood on the cross. The one true religion is Christianity——pure religion, which becomes part of man's very life by embracing the finished work of Jesus——His death on the cross, His burial, His resurrection, His ascension and His return to this earth when the time is ripe. Any man who tries to get to heaven through any other Gospel, by any other way, the same is a thief and a robber (John 10:1). The dirtiest gang of thieves this side of hell is the gang of religious thieves who strip the Word of God and demote Jesus to the level of ordinary men, to prove their religious points and to keep their congregation. According to the verses we have just read, there is *one body* . . . there is only one True Church. There are saved people in many denominations; there are born again people in many local assemblies——but all born again people belong to the one true church——the body of Christ——ONE body. All born again people are members of that body, and when one member suffers, the body suffers.

There is one Spirit . . . ONLY one Spirit. That is the reason we are admonished in the first Epistle of John to try the spirits and be sure the spirit we follow is the Spirit of Jesus and not the spirit of the enemy. You cannot believe every spirit. Many evil spirits are in the world today. You must try the spirits——and any spirit that denies the virgin birth, the blood atonement, the verbal inspiration of the Bible, the reality of sin and damnation ——you mark it and mark it well, that spirit is not the Holy Spirit! On the contrary, it is the spirit of the devil. You be sure you are following the right spirit. Everything having to do with our entrance into the Pearly White City is singular——never plural. One *body*, one *Spirit*, we are called in *one hope* of our calling. Every believer should have a single eye, and that eye should be on Jesus at all times, under all circumstances. Whatever we do, whatever we are, we should have one motive in mind: To glorify the Lord Jesus who left glory and came to earth's sorrow that we might enter glory through His shed blood. God saves us for Christ's sake (Eph. 4:32), and let me remind you that it is only for Christ's sake that God forgives the sinner!

There is *one Lord*. There are many false Christs—but only one Lord and Saviour Jesus Christ . . . just one. We are warned that in the last days there will be many false Christs—and they are here. Many gigantic religious movements are headed by a man or a woman who claims everything the Son of God ever claimed—*except the virgin birth*. (And I am sure that before the Rapture there will be those who will claim to have been born of a virgin.) Cults are spreading like wildfire. It is a sign of the end.

There is one Lord, one faith. You may say, "Preacher, my religion is as good as yours if I am sincere in what I believe." According to the Bible, you are wrong if you say that. If your religion is the Christian religion of salvation by faith in the blood of Jesus Christ, your religion is right. If your religion is anything short of the blood of Jesus Christ and His finished work, you are following a way that will lead you to hell. "There is a way that seemeth right unto a man, but the end thereof are the ways of death" (Prov. 16:25). Regardless of how sincere you may be, your sincerity will never get you inside the Pearly Gates. Faith in the blood of Jesus Christ *will*—one Lord, one Faith, one Baptism! And my precious friend, that is not a baptism in a church baptistry . . . it is the baptism of the Holy Ghost. Each and every one who belongs to the one body has been baptized by the one Spirit, called with the one true calling which is by the Holy Ghost. We have received the one Lord because we have been drawn to Him by the Holy Ghost (John 6:44). We are sons of God because we have exercised the one true faith—faith in the finished work of the one Lord;

143

and we are baptized by the Holy Ghost into the body of Jesus Christ the split second we believe (I Cor. 12:13). Water baptism never saved anyone, and never will save anyone. Yes, it is true that Jesus was baptized. All believers should be baptized. I have been baptized . . . but the one baptism that brings us into the oneness of the body of Christ is not water baptism, but the baptism of the Holy Ghost which occurs when we exercise faith in the finished work of the Lord Jesus Christ.

One God and Father of all. Please notice: *God* and *Father* go together . . . one God and Father of all. No punctuation separates God and Father . . . they are one and the same. Our God is a jealous God (Exodus 20). The Lord Jesus commands, ". . . Call no man your father upon the earth: for one is your Father, which is in heaven" (Matt. 23:9). So you see, dearly beloved, we are to refer to no man in a spiritual sense as our father. We have One God, One Father . . . and He is God and Father of all who are born again.

There is perfect unity in the Godhead, perfect oneness in the Trinity. In our triune God there is no schism. God the Father, God the Son, God the Holy Spirit, are one in providing, planning, and in the working of our salvation. We should demonstrate in our daily living the unity that is demonstrated in the Trinity. It grieves the heart of God when brethren fail to dwell together in perfect harmony and unity. There should be no division among Bible believing Christians, and if the Holy Spirit has His way there will be no division.

THE MINISTRY OF THE NEW TESTAMENT CHURCH

Verses 7–11: "But unto every one of us is given grace according to the measure of the gift of Christ. Wherefore He saith, When He ascended up on high, He

144

led captivity captive, and gave gifts unto men. (Now that He ascended, what is it but that He also descended first into the lower parts of the earth? He that descended is the same also that ascended up far above all heavens, that He might fill all things.) And He gave some, apostles; and some, prophets; and some, evangelists; and some, pastors and teachers."

It will be a victorious day in the lives of some believers when they acknowledge the Bible fact that God is the One who appoints spiritual leaders in the New Testament church, and God gives gifts to individuals according to the measure of their ability. A lot of church division and unrest among believers would not exist if each and every person in the church would allow the Holy Spirit to lead them in what they should do, and if they would allow the Holy Spirit to appoint the leaders in the local assembly. There is entirely too much politics in the church today. Many times people are put into positions of authority because of their social, educational, or monetary standing rather than because of their spiritual standing. I do not say this with a hateful spirit—but if a millionaire is converted, in less than six months he will be on more boards and appointed to more offices than any five men could handle and do the job right. God forbid that I judge—but in many churches the men who have money and social position hold office when some spiritually minded brother who could do the job much better sits idle. I wonder what the Lord Jesus thinks when He looks down upon a situation such as I have just mentioned? Certainly Jesus taught the varying measure of talents in the parables He gave, especially the parables of the talents and the pounds. Study carefully Matthew 25:14–30 and Luke 19:12–27.

Always bear in mind that it is not the quantity (how much you are doing) but the "sort" (the quality) of stewardship, and the spirit with which you discharge your duties. God looks on the heart. God is not concerned with names and fleshly show; He is concerned about fruit that produces results to the glory of God——not to the glory of individuals.

We learn in verses 8 through 10 that Jesus has a perfect right to bestow these gifts upon whom He will, because He is the One who triumphed over all His foes and ours. He conquered what we could never have conquered, from the lowest depths to the highest heights. Jesus "led captivity captive." The evil powers that once held believers captive are now made captive by Christ through His victory over death, hell, and the grave. He now possesses the keys of hell and death (Rev. 1:18). "Forasmuch then as the children are partakers of flesh and blood, He (Jesus) Himself likewise took part of the same (that is, He took the flesh part of man, He did not take man's blood. His blood came from God——Acts 20:28); that through death He might *destroy him that had the power of death*, that is, the devil; AND DELIVER THEM WHO THROUGH FEAR OF DEATH WERE ALL THEIR LIFETIME SUBJECT TO BONDAGE" (Heb. 2:14–15).

Jesus Christ came into this world to take a body of flesh, in order that He might taste death for every man, and through death destroy the devil who then had the power of death. Jesus came to deliver those who lived in fear and bondage because of Satan's power; but now Jesus has the keys of hell and death.

During the earthly ministry of Jesus, the Pharisees asked for a sign. Jesus told them that He would give them only one sign. He said, "An evil and adulterous generation seeketh after a sign; and there shall no sign be given to it, but the sign of the prophet Jonas: For as Jonas was three days and three nights in the whale's belly; SO SHALL THE SON OF MAN BE THREE DAYS AND THREE NIGHTS IN THE HEART OF THE EARTH" (Matt. 12:39–40).

When Jesus died He descended into the Paradise side of hell. At that time Paradise was in the heart of this earth. Jesus actually descended into hell . . . not the torment part of hell; He went into the Paradise side. According to Luke 16 there was a great gulf between the fire, and the Paradise where the righteous were. We read, "For David speaketh concerning Him (Jesus), I foresaw the Lord always before my face, for He is on my right hand, that I should not be moved: Therefore did my heart rejoice, and my tongue was glad; moreover also *my flesh shall rest in hope*, because thou wilt not leave my soul in hell, neither wilt thou suffer thine Holy One to see corruption" (Acts 2:25–27). You will find these same words in Psalm 16:10. These words referred to the Lord Jesus Christ, God's "Holy One."

When Jesus died, His spirit entered into the heart of this earth, and when He arose He brought all of the spirits out of the Paradise in the center of this earth, and carried them with Him to the Paradise far above the first and second heavens. The righteous are now resting with Jesus in the third heaven (II Cor. 12:1–3). It is a clear Bible fact that when a righteous person dies, the spirit goes immediately to be with the Lord. Paul said, "For to me to live is Christ, and to die is gain" (Phil. 1:21). "Therefore we are always confident, knowing that, whilst we are at home in the body, we are absent from the Lord: (for we walk by faith, not by sight:) *We are confident, I say, and willing rather to be absent from the body, and to be present with the Lord.*" (II Cor. 5:6–8).

The doctrine of soul-sleep is foreign to the Word of God. No such doctrine can be found in the Scriptures.

The beggar died and went immediately to Abraham's bosom —the place of rest (the bosom is a symbol of rest . . . a baby rests lying upon the mother's bosom). The beggar went to Paradise. Paul was caught up into Paradise, into the third heaven, and he saw and heard things not lawful to tell on earth (II Cor. 12:1–3). Jesus said to the dying thief who had requested to be remembered by the Lamb of God, "Today shalt thou be with me in Paradise" (Luke 23:43). Regardless of what you have heard or read, to be absent from this body is to be immediately present with the Lord Jesus. He purchased this glorious fact and made possible this glorious provision through His death, burial, and resurrection. Jesus, who ascended far above all heavens after His resurrection, first descended into the lowest part of this earth . . . the heart of the earth. As Jonah spent three days and three nights in the belly of the whale, Jesus spent three days and three nights in the heart of this earth; but He came forth early in the morning, on the third day after His death as He had promised. Many of the saints who came out of Paradise with Him walked the streets in Jerusalem and appeared unto many.

Perhaps someone is asking what happened to those saints after they "appeared to many." The answer is easy: When Jesus went on to the third heaven He carried those saints with Him. But let me give you the Word of God:

"And, behold, the veil of the temple was rent in twain from the top to the bottom; and the earth did quake, and the rocks rent; and the graves were opened and many bodies of the saints which slept arose, and came out of the graves after His resurrection, and went into the holy city, and appeared unto many" (Matt. 27:51–53).

Note: The bodies (not the spirits) slept in the grave. The body goes back to dust, the spirit returns to God who gave it (Eccl. 12:7). The bodies of the saints came

148

out of the graves. The spirits which had been resting in the lower part of this earth entered the bodies——and they walked the streets of Jerusalem, appearing unto many people in that city. Regardless of what any religion or "ism" teaches, the Word of God is clear. Believe it, and junk all else.

Verse 11 needs to be studied and preached in the average local church. Jesus Christ "gave some" . . . that means He appointed, ordained, or set aside individuals for specific ministries. First, apostles. Next, prophets. Then evangelists, and then pastors and teachers. Please notice: The Holy Spirit leaves no untied ends, no unfinished business. The Word of God does not say He gave some "apostles and prophets." There is no connecting conjunction between those two words . . . He did not appoint "apostles and prophets" as one. He did not appoint "prophets and evangelists" or "apostles and evangelists." He appoints individuals to specific ministries until he reaches the most important appointee (or worker) in the New Testament church: Pastors and teachers. A pastor can be a good, efficient pastor and a teacher. But dearly beloved, I do not believe there is an evangelist on the face of this earth who, if he is a God-called, God-sent evangelist, can successfully pastor a church, teach the people and lead them into the deeper spiritual experiences set forth in Paul's letter to the church at Ephesus. An evangelist has a specific and peculiar ministry. Sad but so, most churches have completely outlawed evangelists. I realize that in some cases this is justified. There have been (and still are) evangelists who are not what they should be by any means—— but not all evangelists are counterfeits. There are some pastors who are not what they should be——but we cannot judge all pastors by those who are not God's pastors. The same is true in the ministry of the evangelist.

149

The apostles are all gone---Paul was the last. We have no prophets in the church today. The entire New Testament is ours, we have received the perfect law of liberty (the entire Word of God). In I Corinthians 13:10 Paul tells us ". . . When that which is perfect is come, then that which is in part shall be done away." The apostles performed their ministry; the prophets performed their ministry. Today God is using evangelists, pastors and teachers to carry on the work of the ministry in the church.

A New Testament church should have at least three special meetings each year:

1. A Bible Conference--where Bible teachers (not evangelists) should be brought in . . . deep men of God, seasoned men of God---men who have been with God and are capable of teaching.

2. An Evangelistic Campaign. A Bible teacher should not be called in to conduct evangelistic meetings. God's evangelist should be brought in . . . a man who can stir the people with the pure Word of God. An evangelist has a singular ministry. He is not called of God to teach deep spiritual truths. He is called to stir the people.

3. A Missionary Conference. God's missionaries should be brought in to enlighten the people in regard to the field of missions. Sometimes a missionary-evangelist may be used . . . or just a teacher from a mission school. Perhaps a doctor or a nurse from a mission hospital might be called in. The missionary speakers should be missionaries---not pastors, not evangelists on the home front . . . but missionaries from the foreign field. If we are to have a missionary conference, missionaries should be the speakers at that conference.

Since a grocery store sells groceries, certainly a filling station sign should not be hung over the door; and if we are having a Bible conference, it should be held by men who know the Word of God and who are capable of teaching the Word of God. If we advertise a missionary conference, we should have a missionary conference; and people who attend should hear a message on missions, delivered by someone who knows what he is talking about. When we advertise an evangelistic campaign, we should hear an evangelistic message.

This is God's program—but sad to say, in too many churches today God does not have anything to do with the program. The pastor, the board of deacons, trustees, and committees draw up the program, and they choose the speaker they want. They do not let God Almighty have any part in it. I am not judging. I have been traveling for many years and I have learned a few things in the years I have been in the evangelistic ministry.

Yes, it pleased God to set in the church apostles, prophets, evangelists, pastors and teachers; and if churches are to follow the New Testament pattern in conducting their services, that is the pattern they should follow.

THE PURPOSE OF
THE MINISTRY OF THE APPOINTED SERVANTS

Verses 12–16: "For the perfecting of the saints, for the work of the ministry, for the edifying of the body of Christ: till we all come in the unity of the faith, and of the knowledge of the Son of God, unto a perfect man, unto the measure of the stature of the fulness of Christ: That we henceforth be no more children, tossed to and fro, and carried about with every wind of doctrine, by the sleight of men, and cunning craftiness, whereby they lie in wait to deceive; But speaking the truth in love, may grow up into Him in all things, which is the head, even Christ: From whom the whole body fitly joined together

151

and compacted by that which every joint supplieth, according to the effectual working in the measure of every part, maketh increase of the body unto the edifying of itself in love."

I would like to point out three things in verses 12 and 13. God appoints these different servants (or ministers) for:

1. The perfecting of the saints
2. The work of the ministry
3. The edifying of the body of Christ

This is to continue until "we all come in the unity of the faith and the knowledge of the Son of God unto a perfect man, unto the measure of the stature of the fulness of Christ." In other words, God calls, appoints, commissions and sends ministers into the local assembly for the perfecting of the saints, for the work of the ministry, for the edifying of the body of Christ, *uniting all believers in the faith.* God does not send in men who will divide the church by setting forth some new doctrine, man-made dogma, or an idea that is hatched up by some committee at the headquarters of a religious denomination. God sends spiritually minded ministers who are able to lead the people of God into the deeper things of the spirit in order that the body of the local church may grow into a full grown spiritual man in Christ Jesus——which is what we should be.

The Lord calls and sends gifted men (as in Acts 11:22–26, Acts 13:1–2, Acts 16:6–7). The ministry of pastors, teachers and evangelists is not according to human choosing or sending. If the church is a New Testament church the Holy Spirit appoints men to the ministry or places of service there. The Holy Spirit may direct some young man to a needy community where there is no Bible church, to organize and pastor a Bible-believing church there. Many young men would be led to places of service if they would look to the Holy Spirit for leadership, instead of to the denomination or to the home church. Too many times in this day young ministers wait for the denomination to provide a place for them to preach. God's ministers do not pick out the place they would like to go——and then go there; a Spirit-led minister is not permitted to choose his own place of service. (Read Acts 16:7–8.)

Paul begs the Ephesians not to be like children, tossed to and fro, carried around with every wind of doctrine and by the sleight of men who lie in wait to deceive by cunning craftiness. This is good sound advice and is badly needed in our churches today. The average church has entirely too many spiritual babies still being bottle-fed. Paul told the Corinthians they should be eating meat——but were still feeding on milk because they were carnal. They were divided, they were criticizing, they were back-biting. One declared, "Apollos baptized me," another said, "Cephas baptized me." They were fighting among themselves, therefore they had no time left in which to fight the devil. Paul rebuked them for this——and rightly so. He admonished the Ephesians to grow up . . . not to remain spiritual babies, not be children tossed about by every wind of doctrine.

Believers should study the Word of God, hear the man of God, discover the doctrine of the Bible, stand on it, live by it, die by it if necessary——and do not allow deceivers to get into the assembly . . . wolves in sheep's clothing to lead the lambs astray. A good shepherd takes care of the lambs and the sheep in his fold.

The average pastor who is driven away from his church has no one but himself to blame. Beloved, if a pastor is called of God and ordained of God, he is the

153

undershepherd of Almighty God. God furnishes the shells with which to shell the woods. God furnishes the tools and the ammunition. If a preacher allows heresy and false doctrine to creep into his church, it is his own fault. If he is alert, if he brings in the right Bible teachers, the right missionaries and the right evangelists . . . men who will preach pure, sound doctrine . . . the church will not be led about with every "wind of doctrine."

The gross ignorance concerning doctrine in the average church is sad beyond human knowledge. The average church member does not know what he believes; and what little he does believe, he does not know why he believes it. I say this in love: Many churches do not have three people in their entire membership who could take the Word of God and instruct a sinner how to be saved! Brethren, that should not be! God pity the pastor who does not ground his people in the doctrine of the Word of God.

Paul believed in Dynamics, Discipline, and Doctrine. He had three "D's" . . . he was not just D.D. He was Dynamic, he believed in Discipline——and he preached sound Doctrine. If a dear minister hopes to keep his church the kind of church that would please the Lord, he must himself preach sound doctrine, teach the people, train them, and lead them. He must be extremely careful whom he brings in to minister to the people. When a pastor leaves his pulpit he must be extremely cautious about who fills that pulpit in his absence. In one hour, a false prophet can sow seed that will bring shame upon the church for months and months to come.

It is sad today that many times in the church some dear soul who seems to have been stable and grounded in the faith is swept off his feet by some new religious idea that sweeps through town. That ought not to be. God's minister does not change his message with the times. A Christian who is established on the Rock Christ Jesus will not be confused, confounded, nor led astray by false doctrine. Is there Scripture to prove that? Yes:

"Wherefore also it is contained in the Scripture, Behold, I lay in Sion a chief corner stone (Jesus is the Rock), elect, precious: AND HE THAT BELIEVETH ON HIM SHALL NOT BE CONFOUNDED" (I Peter 2:6). That verse of Scripture needs no comment. Jesus is the Rock, and if we are standing on the sure foundation, the spiritual Rock of Gibraltar, the Lord Jesus Christ, we will not be confused, confounded, nor driven about by divers winds of doctrine. God pity these wind-cloud Christians.

Jude refers to clouds driven by the wind, people who are twice dead, plucked up by the roots . . . church members, but with no stability, no grounded experience. They are tossed about, and change their religion and their doctrine every so often.

Earlier in this study I pointed out that there is a difference—and yet there is no difference—in the ministry of the pastor and the evangelist, the teacher and the evangelist. A pastor can be (and should be) a pastor AND a teacher, because no pastor can be an effective pastor unless he is capable of teaching . . . and teaching requires much study and prayer. An evangelist should be a teacher to some degree—because if we cannot teach the Word and make plain the plan of salvation, we cannot evangelize. But the number one ministry of the evangelist is to edify and stir up, and cause the unsaved as well as the believers to think on their eternal destiny. When an evangelist comes into a church, he does not preach a new Gospel . . . he just preaches the same old Gospel in a different way, to stir up the saints and get them busy, to cause them to work. The pastor, the evangelist, the teacher, each and every minister in the New Testament church certainly works to the same end . . . the perfecting of the saints . . . the perfecting of the body . . . the completion of the church.

Certainly an evangelist should have in mind adding souls to the body of Christ through the preaching of the Gospel; and the pastor should also desire through the teaching of the Gospel to add souls and to strengthen the babes in Christ and to feed the stronger Christians . . . those who are eating meat. The Christian experience is a day-by-day process. We are redeemed instantaneously —but we grow in grace and in the knowledge of our Lord and Saviour Jesus Christ. As new-born babes we are commanded to desire the sincere milk of the Word that we may grow. We are to study to show ourselves approved unto God, workmen that need not be ashamed. The sad condition of most Christians is that they are saved, and they bog down spiritually, never moving forward. They are spiritual dwarfs. They have spiritual anemia. They are undernourished, they do not grow. It is sad. It should not be.

We are to teach, preach, edify, stir up the people. We are to cause the sinner to be saved through the Gospel, and the Christian to grow through the milk, meat, bread and water of the Word. Sometimes I shudder when I think that one day I will stand before Almighty God to give an account for my labors in the body. I am redeemed by the blood—but I will be rewarded according to my faithful labors; and I wonder if I have been faithful at all times? I wonder if I have done all that I could? God pity us if we are not faithful ministers of the Gospel!

We are to speak the truth in love—we are not to speak the truth with hatefulness or sarcasm, but in love. Ministers are never to apologize for preaching the truth.

We (evangelists, pastors, teachers) should step into the pulpit and tell people "except a man be born again he cannot see the kingdom of God . . . if any man love the world the love of God is not in him . . . except ye repent ye shall all likewise perish . . . he that climbeth up some other way the same is a thief and a robber . . . Jesus is the way, the truth and the life . . . no man can come to God the Father but by Jesus the Son . . . there is only one Mediator between God and men, the Man Christ Jesus . . . the wages of sin is death." When we preach these things we need not apologize nor soft-pedal such truth. We need to preach it with positiveness, we need to be dogmatic . . . but we need to do it in love.

Verse 15 closes with the words, ". . . into Him in all things, which is the head, even Christ." Then verse 16 begins, "From whom the whole body fitly joined together and compacted by that which every joint supplieth . . . ."

The church of the living God, the church of which Jesus is the head, is a body made up of living organisms . . . individuals who are born again. We are not all eyes, we are not all hands, we are not all feet; but we are ALL members of one body. Paul explains to the Corinthian believers in these words:

"For as the body is one, and hath many members, and all the members of that one body, being many, are one body: so also is Christ." (Paul is using the natural body to illustrate the church. Certainly we know what the physical body is, how it is made up, and how necessary are all the members of it.) "For by one Spirit are we all baptized into one body (all believers), whether we be Jews or Gentiles, whether we be bond or free; and have been all made to drink into one Spirit. For the body (the church) is not one member, but many."

Paul then begins to point out the different members

as compared to the human body: "If the foot shall say, Because I am not the hand, I am not of the body; is it therefore not of the body? And if the ear shall say, Because I am not the eye, I am not of the body; is it therefore not of the body? If the whole body were an eye, where were the hearing? If the whole were hearing, where were the smelling? But now hath God set the members every one of them in the body, as it hath pleased Him."

(You will note here that it is *God* who places individuals in specific ministries in the church; and if we as individuals would be so surrendered to God that we would allow Him to place us where He wants us, we would be happy and fruitful.)

"And if they were all one member, where were the body? But now are they many members, yet but one body (still speaking of the church). And the eye cannot say unto the hand, I have no need of thee: nor again the head to the feet, I have no need of you. Nay, much more THOSE MEMBERS OF THE BODY, WHICH SEEM TO BE MORE FEEBLE, ARE NECESSARY: AND THOSE MEMBERS OF THE BODY, WHICH WE THINK TO BE LESS HONOURABLE, UPON THESE WE BESTOW MORE ABUNDANT HONOUR; AND OUR UNCOMELY PARTS HAVE MORE ABUNDANT COMELINESS. For our comely parts have no need: but God hath tempered the body together, having given more abundant honour to that part which lacked: that there should be no schism in the body; but that the members should have the same care one for another. And whether one member suffer, ALL THE MEMBERS SUFFER WITH IT; OR ONE MEMBER BE HONOURED, ALL THE MEMBERS REJOICE WITH IT. NOW YE ARE THE BODY OF CHRIST, AND MEMBERS IN PARTICULAR" (I Cor. 12:12–27).

In these verses we clearly see that each and every

born again child of God is a member of the one church of the living God . . . the body of Christ. And regardless of how humble may be the ministry of each individual in that body, we are important. There are no unimportant parts in the New Testament church. Your ministry may be very, very humble––but remember, God places more honor upon the humble. One of the greatest surprises of eternity will be at the judgment seat of Christ where believers will be rewarded for their stewardship. Those who seemingly would have received great rewards will many times be those who receive a very small reward, while some dear soul who was very insignificant on this earth will receive a great reward in heaven, because God will reward for faithfulness––not for the size of the ministry (I Cor. 3:11–15, II Cor. 5:10).

To sum it all up, from the pastor to the janitor in the church, every person should be united, working toward one end: The perfecting of the saints, the edifying of the body until the church is complete and we are caught out to meet Jesus in the clouds in the air (I Thess. 4: 13–18).

BELIEVERS ARE NEW CREATIONS IN CHRIST– WE ARE TO WALK AS A NEW MAN

Verses 17–19: "This I say therefore, and testify in the Lord, that ye henceforth walk not as other Gentiles walk, in the vanity of their mind, having the understanding darkened, being alienated from the life of God through the ignorance that is in them, because of the blindness of their heart: Who being past feeling have given themselves over unto lasciviousness, to work all uncleanness with greediness."

Born again believers, members of the body of Christ, are new creations. A believer is a new man; therefore, we are to put off the clothing, the garments (the life), of the old man and put on the new man. In I Corinthians 2:14–15, and in I Corinthians 3:1 we read concerning the natural man, the carnal man, and the spiritual man. There are believers who deny that there is such a person as a carnal Christian. To make that statement from the pulpit is to invite some people to call the minister or evangelist a false prophet; but I am not a false prophet: "But the natural man receiveth not the things of the Spirit of God: for they are foolishness unto him: neither can he know them, because they are spiritually discerned" (I Cor. 2:14). The natural man CANNOT receive the things of God because his heart is dead, his mind is blinded by the god of this age, and he cannot receive the things of the Spirit of God.

"But he that is spiritual judgeth all things, yet he himself is judged of no man" (I Cor. 2:15). This second man is spiritual and he judges all things—yet he himself is judged of no man because the spiritual man gives an account to God, not to his fellowman. We will be judged of the Lord, and we are to judge nothing before the time.

So—we have two men—the natural man and the spiritual man: "And I, brethren, could not speak unto you as unto spiritual, but as unto carnal, even as unto babes in Christ. I have fed you with milk, and not with meat: for hitherto ye were not able to bear it, neither yet now are ye able. FOR YE ARE YET CARNAL: for whereas there is among you envying, and strife, and divisions, ARE YE NOT CARNAL, AND WALK AS MEN? For while one saith, I am of Paul; and another, I am of Apollos; ARE YE NOT CARNAL?" (I Cor. 3:1–4).

Thus, in the last verses of chapter two and the first verses of chapter three of I Corinthians, we are clearly taught that we have three distinct men on earth today:

(1) the natural man who needs to be born again, (2) the spiritual man who has been born of the Spirit, and (3) the carnal man who is a babe in Christ, feeding on milk because of carnality described as envyings, strife, divisions—and bragging about the fact that some outstanding evangelist is the one who baptized him.

We had as well face it, there is no need to deny it: *All born again people possess the Holy Ghost, but all born again people are not spiritual.* All born again people are not filled with the Spirit (Eph. 5:18). Yes, there are born again people who are carnal. They have not grown, they are still babes. In the preceding verses in our study in Ephesians, Paul said, "Be no more children, tossed to and fro." God wants us to grow up. Sad but true, many Christians seemingly will never grow up. The dear pastor has a hard job. He has the spiritually minded in his church who need meat . . . strong meat; they love meat and crave it. But he also has the babes who are on milk, and they are not able to bear the meat. So God's dear preacher has a problem when he goes into the pulpit to feed the children of God.

Verses 17, 18, and 19 give us the picture of the unregenerate, and we are not to walk as sinners walk. By nature, the unregenerate has a mind filled with vanity. His understanding is darkened. The heart of the natural man is blind. He has no feeling toward God, he is given over to lasciviousness, working all uncleanness with greediness.

Paul gives a picture of the unregenerate in Titus 3:3: "For we ourselves also were sometimes foolish, disobedient, deceived, serving divers lusts and pleasures, living in malice and envy, hateful, and hating one another." In connection with this, read Romans 1:21–32 and you will get a full-sized, sordid, despicable portrait

161

and the life-sized features of an unregenerated man. We who are new creations in Christ Jesus are not to walk as these men walk. We are to put off the carnal man because we have "NOT SO LEARNED CHRIST." We who know Christ have not been taught such an evil practice of life. We are to live a new life because we are a new creation in Christ Jesus. We know THE TRUTH IN CHRIST; and we should follow His teaching as the example of our daily living. David describes it in these words: "The Lord is my shepherd . . . HE LEADETH ME IN THE PATHS OF RIGHTEOUSNESS (right living) FOR HIS NAME'S SAKE" (Psalm 23).

When we are born again we are called upon to "put off" the old garments of the natural life, the natural man. We are to deny the ways of the "old man." (The "old man" is by nature corrupt, and by nature follows "deceitful lust.") As many as are led by the Spirit of God are the sons of God, and if we walk in the Spirit we will not fulfill the lusts of the flesh. If we love the world, the love of God is not in us. The grace of God that brings salvation teaches us to deny ungodliness, to deny worldly lusts, and to live sober, righteous lives in this present age . . . looking for and hastening to . . . "the glorious appearing of the great God and our Saviour, Jesus Christ."

Verses 20–29: "But ye have not so learned Christ; if so be that ye have heard Him, and been taught by Him, as the truth is in Jesus: That ye put off concerning the former conversation the old man, which is corrupt according to the deceitful lusts; and be renewed in the spirit of your mind; and that ye put on the new man, which after God is created in righteousness and true holiness. Wherefore putting away lying, speak every man truth with his neighbour: for we are members one of another. Be ye angry, and sin not: let not the sun go down upon your wrath: Neither give place to the devil. Let him that stole steal no more: but rather let him labour, working with his hands the thing which is good, that he may have to give to him that needeth. Let no corrupt communication proceed out of your mouth, but that which is good to the use of edifying, that it may minister grace unto the hearers."

According to Greek authorities there is a mis-translation in verse 21. It should not read "as the truth is IN Jesus." In the Greek there is no preposition "in." The phrase should read, "As the truth is JESUS." That is exactly what Jesus said to Thomas: "I am the *Way*, the *Truth*, and the *Life*. No man cometh to the Father but by me" (John 14:6). The truth is not IN Jesus; Jesus IS the Truth. There is no truth apart from Jesus. He does not just "possess the truth," He does not just "tell the truth." He is the Truth. It is impossible for Jesus to lie. When He speaks, His words are spirit and truth (John 6:63, John 1:1, John 1:14, Heb. 6:18 and Titus 1:2).

"Ye shall know the truth, and the truth shall make you free" (John 8:32).

"If the Son therefore shall make you free, ye shall be free indeed" (John 8:36). Jesus is the truth, and in Jesus we have all spiritual blessings . . . but ONLY in Jesus.

In verses 23 and following, we are instructed to put on the spiritual man. Christians belong to a new order, a new creation, we are a new man. The first step in spiritual things is not to be repaired or overhauled—but "renewed." We must become a new creation through the miracle of the new birth. The new birth occurs through the power of the Gospel and the operation of the Holy Spirit. Therefore, we are redeemed through the power of God. We become a new creation (II Cor. 5:17, II Peter 1:4). We are renewed in soul, spirit, mind and heart. We are to be renewed "in the spirit of (the) mind." The mind must think right about God before we can trust Him fully. When we think right concerning God, Christ, the Word, and the Holy Spirit, then we can walk in the newness of life——but not until we have been renewed in our minds by the power of God. God does not work on the surface . . . on the outside; He works on the inside.

In verse 24 we note that the "new man" is "after God." The new man is a product of God's power to create a new man——not to repair the old man. We are created in Christ Jesus, as we learned in Ephesians 2:10. We are created "in righteousness and true holiness." Notice the first word in verse 25: "WHEREFORE." That means, "Because of the preceding, the following is true." Wherefore (or because) we have put on the new man, we are a new creation, created in Christ Jesus by the miracle and the power of the Holy Ghost. Because of this miracle in our life, we are to put away, to put off . . . "LYING."

In verse 21 we learned that Jesus is Truth; and truth and lying have no place in the same heart. A truthful heart is not a lying heart, and a lying heart does not possess truth. Therefore, when truth comes in, lying automatically falls off. Jesus is Truth. Satan is the lie. The first thing named to be dropped by the new man is "lying."

We are to put away anger, we are to put away stealing, we are to be honest in our labors and purpose of life. We are to work in order that we might have means to help those who are less fortunate than we are. We are to put away worthless, foolish talk. We are not to say things that would deny the new man within, or misrepresent the new creation. Our conversation should always be such as to edify, build up, strengthen . . . never to tear down and hinder other Christians or stand in the way of sinners. We are always to be "ministering grace to the hearers." We are to put away all that grieves the Spirit, remembering that He abides in our bosom at all times, and if we say things, do things, go places, and keep company that grieves the Spirit, certainly that is wrong.

Let me point out some things about anger. Perhaps you do not understand the statement, "Be ye angry and sin not. Let not the sun go down upon your wrath." The believer can indulge in "RIGHTEOUS INDIGNATION" without sinning. There are times when, in the pulpit, I become very angry; but it is the right kind of anger. I am angry at the devil, at sin. When I am preaching against the liquor crowd . . . men who would sell liquor to your eighteen year old boy or your sixteen year old girl, thus causing them to commit sin that would wreck their life and ruin them . . . I am angry with those men. . . . But I would put my arm around any one of them and lead him to Jesus if he would give me the chance. We can be extremely angry——and yet not sin. A minister who cannot GET ANGRY in the pulpit is not worth two cents! I do not mean become angry at souls who need Jesus. I mean become angry at sin . . . because of the fruits of iniquity. A minister needs the ability to become righteously indignant——and yet not sin.

In Galatians 5:19—21 it is clearly taught that anger is the working of the flesh——but that is another kind of anger . . . not righteous indignation.

Verses 30—32: "And grieve not the Holy Spirit of God, whereby ye are sealed unto the day of redemption. Let all bitterness, and wrath, and anger, and clamour, and evil speaking, be put away from you, with all malice: And be ye kind one to another, tenderhearted, forgiving one another, even as God for Christ's sake hath forgiven you."

165

Let me give you a brief outline of the Holy Spirit's part in our redemption and in our journey to the Pearly White City:

1. First, we are drawn to God by the power of the Holy Ghost (John 6:44, John 16:7–11).

2. The Holy Spirit "borns" us into God's family (John 1:11–13, John 3:5–7). The Holy Spirit is the attending physician at the spiritual birth which occurs through the Word (John 5:24, Eph. 2:8–9, Rom. 10:17, I Pet. 1:23).

3. At the time of the new birth the Holy Spirit baptizes us into the body of Christ (I Cor. 12:12–13).

4. The Holy Spirit of God seals us until the day of redemption (Eph. 4:30). The Holy Ghost puts upon our heart the stamp of God's ownership, and the seal remains until the Holy Spirit performs His last work in our journey from redemption to the Pearly White City.

5. The Holy Spirit leads us into the paths of right living (Rom. 8:9, Rom. 8:14, Gal. 5:16, Psalm 23:1–3).

6. When we allow the Holy Spirit, He fills us (Eph. 5:18–20).

7. We shall be quickened by the Spirit in the first resurrection, which will occur at the Rapture of the church: "But if the Spirit of Him that raised up Jesus from the dead dwell in you, HE THAT RAISED UP CHRIST FROM THE DEAD SHALL ALSO QUICKEN (make alive) YOUR MORTAL BODIES BY HIS SPIRIT THAT DWELLETH IN YOU" (Rom. 8:11). Read carefully I Corinthians 15:35–57. You will note that this passage of Scripture begins with a question: "But some man will say, How are the dead raised up? and with what body do they come?" Later in the chapter, the Holy Spirit reveals, "It is sown a natural body; it is raised a spiritual body. There is a natural body, and there is a spiritual body. And so it is

166

written, The first man Adam was made a living soul; THE LAST ADAM WAS MADE A QUICKENING SPIRIT. Howbeit that was not first which is spiritual, but that which is natural; and afterward that which is spiritual."

"For Christ also hath once suffered for sins, the just for the unjust, that He might bring us to God, being put to death in the flesh, but quickened by the Spirit" (I Peter 3:18).

In the first resurrection (I Thess. 4:13–18, I Cor. 15:51–55) the bodies of the saints who have died will be quickened (made alive) by the power of the Holy Spirit. The living bodies will be changed by the Spirit in the twinkling of an eye . . . in the fraction of a split second. The Holy Ghost will see us safely inside the Pearly Gates. I am so glad Jesus did not save me and put me on board the salvation ship––and then say, "Son, work hard; strive and endure to the bitter end; do your best. I hope you do not run into any storms; I hope there will be no pitfalls in your path. I wish you well. Do your best to make it to heaven." I am glad the Bible does not say that! But rather, God's precious Holy Word says this: "I will never leave thee nor forsake thee . . . We may boldly say, God is my helper . . . There hath no temptation taken you but such as is common to every man–– but God is faithful, who will not permit you to be tempted above that ye are able, but will with the very temptation make a way for you to escape . . . Ye have overcome them because greater (more powerful) is Jesus in you than Satan in the world!"

We are more than conquerors through Christ who loved us. My God shall supply all your needs––physical, financial, mental, spiritual . . . whatsoever the need . . . THROUGH HIS RICHES IN GLORY BY CHRIST JESUS. God the Father loved us so much that He gave God the

Son to die for us on the cruel cross. God the Son died for us, descended into the lower parts of this earth, conquered death, hell and the grave; ascended from the dead with the keys to death, hell and the grave, appeared to chosen men of God (five hundred at one time). He ascended back to the Father, and on the day of Pentecost He sent the Holy Spirit . . . and He (the Holy Spirit) has been in the world ever since then, to convict the sinner, to draw the sinner, to "born" the sinner; to indwell the believer, to baptize him into the body of Christ, lead him into the paths of righteousness and around the pitfalls of the devil. The Holy Spirit has been here to fill those of us who will permit Him to fill us; and He is our seal of ownership. Every true, blood-washed believer has God's stamp of ownership on his or her heart; and the Spirit will not forget us if we depart this life and the body goes back to dust. He will quicken our flesh and give us a brand new body just like the glorious body of Jesus!

Behold what manner of love! . . . It doth not yet appear exactly what we will be, BUT WE KNOW THAT WHEN JESUS COMES WE SHALL BE LIKE HIM! (I John 3:1–3).

Paul begs the believers at Ephesus not to grieve the Holy Spirit of God. It is possible for a believer to grieve the Spirit. It is possible for us to quench the Spirit. Paul tells us, "Quench not the Spirit" (I Thess. 5:19). We should realize and recognize the Bible fact that our bodies are the temple of the Holy Spirit, and we should be careful how we treat Him. He is a person just as surely as God the Father and God the Son are persons. God the Father is a person, God the Son is a person—and in like manner the Holy Spirit is a person. He can be grieved, He can be quenched. We should be very careful how we treat the Spirit who abides in our bosom.

168

In verse 31, we are told to put aside all bitterness, all wrath, all anger, clamor and evil speaking, and we are to put away all malice. We are to be kind to each other, we are to be tender-hearted. Jesus was tender-hearted and we are to follow His steps. We are to be Christ-like if we advertise to the world that we are Christians. Insofar as is humanly possible, we are to live as our Christ lived when He was on this earth. We should have a forgiving spirit——why? Because . . . "God for Christ's sake hath forgiven you."

There is a tremendous truth here: Dear reader, if you are saved, you are saved for the same reason I am saved. God did not save you or me because we were fit to be saved, nor because we were good enough to be saved. God saved us *for Christ's sake*. Through the Holy Ghost, God is forming a bride for His Son, made up of individuals who put their faith in Jesus. God did not save us just so we would have a happy life on this earth. God did not save us just so we would go to heaven when we die, and not burn in hell. God saved us *for Jesus' sake*, for the joy and the glory of His only begotten Son. For an inheritance to the only begotten Son, we born again believers will be displayed in the heavenlies to show the exceeding riches of God's grace, as we learned in Ephesians chapter two. In case you have a tendency to be just a little bit "puffed up" because of your sonship in the family of God, proud of your spirituality and holiness, just remember that the only reason you are not dead and in hell——or on the road to hell——is because God for Christ's sake saved you! Had it not been for the willingness of Jesus to lay His life down, the willingness of the Holy Spirit to draw you and convict you while you were yet ungodly . . . had it not been for the sake of the only begotten Son of God, you would not be saved——and no sinner would ever have been saved. God saves sinners "FOR CHRIST'S SAKE."

1. Be ye therefore followers of God, as dear children;

2. And walk in love, as Christ also hath loved us, and hath given himself for us an offering and a sacrifice to God for a sweetsmelling savour.

3. But fornication, and all uncleanness, or covetousness, let it not be once named among you, as becometh saints;

4. Neither filthiness, nor foolish talking, nor jesting, which are not convenient: but rather giving of thanks.

5. For this ye know, that no whoremonger, nor unclean person, nor covetous man, who is an idolater, hath any inheritance in the kingdom of Christ and of God.

6. Let no man deceive you with vain words: for because of these things cometh the wrath of God upon the children of disobedience.

7. Be not ye therefore partakers with them.

8. For ye were sometimes darkness, but now are ye light in the Lord: walk as children of light:

9. (For the fruit of the Spirit is in all goodness and righteousness and truth;)

10. Proving what is acceptable unto the Lord.

11. And have no fellowship with the unfruitful works of darkness, but rather reprove them.

12. For it is a shame even to speak of those things which are done of them in secret.

13. But all things that are reproved are made manifest by the light: for whatsoever doth make manifest is light.

14. Wherefore he saith, Awake thou that sleepest, and arise from the dead, and Christ shall give thee light.

15. See then that ye walk circumspectly, not as fools, but as wise,

16. Redeeming the time, because the days are evil.

17. Wherefore be ye not unwise, but understanding what the will of the Lord is.

18. And be not drunk with wine, wherein is excess; but be filled with the Spirit;

19. Speaking to yourselves in psalms and hymns and spiritual songs, singing and making melody in your heart to the Lord;

20. Giving thanks always for all things unto God and the Father in the name of our Lord Jesus Christ;

21. Submitting yourselves one to another in the fear of God.

22. Wives, submit yourselves unto your own husbands, as unto the Lord.

23. For the husband is the head of the wife, even as Christ is the head of the church: and he is the saviour of the body.

24. Therefore as the church is subject unto Christ, so let the wives be to their own husbands in every thing.

25. Husbands, love your wives, even as Christ also loved the church, and gave himself for it;

26. That he might sanctify and cleanse it with the washing of water by the word,

27. That he might present it to himself a glorious church, not having spot, or wrinkle, or any such thing; but that it should be holy and without blemish.

28. So ought men to love their wives as their own bodies. He that loveth his wife loveth himself.

29. For no man ever yet hated his own flesh; but nourisheth and cherisheth it, even as the Lord the church:

30. For we are members of his body, of his flesh, and of his bones.

31. For this cause shall a man leave his father and mother, and shall be joined unto his wife, and they two shall be one flesh.

32. This is a great mystery: but I speak concerning Christ and the church.

33. Nevertheless let every one of you in particular so love his wife even as himself; and the wife see that she reverence her husband.

AS GOD'S CHILD WE SHOULD FOLLOW GOD
IN THE SAME FASHION
AS OUR CHILDREN FOLLOW US

Verses 1 and 2: "Be ye therefore followers of God, as dear children; and walk in love, as Christ also hath loved us, and hath given Himself for us an offering and a sacrifice to God for a sweetsmelling savour."

How well do I remember when my sons (who are young men now) were little boys . . . my little children. They would go everywhere I went if they were allowed to do so; they followed in my steps. I am sure you have heard the story of the drunkard who was on his way to the saloon to get a drink early one morning after a beautiful snow had fallen the night before. As he walked through the snow, his feet made imprints there. He had a little boy about four years old . . . the apple of his eye, the joy of his life. He loved that little boy more than he loved his own life. He had not gone far when he heard someone crunching in the snow behind him. When he

171

turned to look, it was his little son. The boy was stretching his little legs as far as he possibly could, taking long steps. The father said, "Son, what on earth are you doing?" The boy replied, "Daddy, I am stepping in your tracks!" The story goes that instead of going to the saloon, the father picked up the little boy in his arms, pulled him close, wrapped his coat around the shivering little body and returned home, never to enter a saloon again. Why? Because his little boy was walking in his footsteps.

As children of God, we should walk in His steps. Let me point out something here that needs to be noted: We have two extremes today . . . we have the liberals, and the legalizers. We have those who shout "Grace," but put their members under Law. We are not to walk in the footsteps of Jesus because we are afraid not to. We are not to give up bad habits because the church doctrine or dogma declares that we are not to go certain places or do certain things. If you give up a filthy habit because that is the rule in your church, then God gets no glory and you will gain no eternal profit by giving up the habit; but if you give up the lust of the flesh and the habits of the world because you love Jesus, if you stay out of the spiritual saloons (things that would cause you not to be a sober, temperate Christian) because you love Jesus, then you will be blessed, the body will be blessed, and heaven will gain because of your sacrificial living in love.

Born again children of God are:

1. *Children of love*—because our spiritual Father is love. We are begotten of God; therefore we are children of love. "God is love" (I John 4:8).

2. *Children of light.* Our Heavenly Father is light. We are begotten of God; therefore we are the children of light. "God is light" (John 1:4–5; I Thess. 5:4–7).

172

3. *Children of wisdom*. Our God and our Christ are wisdom. We are begotten of God and we abide in Christ; therefore we are the children of wisdom (Prov. 1:7; I Cor. 1:29–31).

In the Sermon on the Mount, Jesus said to His disciples; ". . . I say unto you, LOVE YOUR ENEMIES, bless them that curse you, do good to them that hate you, and pray for them which despitefully use you, and persecute you; THAT YE MAY BE THE CHILDREN OF YOUR FATHER WHICH IS IN HEAVEN: for He maketh His sun to rise on the evil and on the good, and sendeth rain on the just and on the unjust" (Matt. 5:44–45).

If God treated mankind like some Christians treat each other . . . and like some Christians treat their sinner neighbors and friends . . . this earth would be a place of untold agony. Jesus loved His enemies . . . He did not compromise with them, He did not love their sin, but He loved *them*. The essence of Christianity is love, and if we do not love our fellowman whom we see, how can we love God whom we cannot see? We love Him . . . because He first loved us, and if we are born again . . . spiritually minded as we ought to be . . . we will display love in our daily living.

True love is two-fold, as set forth here:

1. True love denies self. Jesus the very Son of God was rich but for our sakes became poor. He took a body —and in that body He suffered, bled and died. He denied Himself . . . "Not my will, but thine be done." He said, "I came not to do my will, but the will of the Father." He never performed any miracle for selfish reasons. The love of Jesus is self-denying. He gave His life, His all. He gave up all for us; we should be willing to give up all for Him.

2. Jesus sacrificed all, and gave Himself an offering

173

to God "FOR A SWEETSMELLING SAVOUR " The sacrifice Jesus made gratified (or pleased) God. Three times in an audible voice God said, "This is my beloved Son in whom I am well pleased" . . . "This is my beloved Son in whom I am well pleased; hear ye Him" . . . "I have glorified thy name, and I will glorify thy name on the earth." As I said earlier in the message, if we do not sacrifice because we love Jesus then our sacrificial living, abstaining, and doing does not glorify God and is of no eternal value.

Verses 3–7: "But fornication, and all uncleanness, or covetousness, let it not be once named among you, as becometh saints; neither filthiness, nor foolish talking, nor jesting, which are not convenient: but rather giving of thanks. For this ye know, that no whoremonger, nor unclean person, nor covetous man, who is an idolater, hath any inheritance in the kingdom of Christ and of God. Let no man deceive you with vain words: for because of these things cometh the wrath of God upon the children of disobedience. Be not ye therefore partakers with them."

The filthy lusts of the flesh named in these verses are not to be mentioned among the saints of God. Of course, fornication and sensual sins come from selfishness, self-seeking and self-gratification on the part of the individual. Such a life is certainly the exact opposite of a life of love, righteousness and holiness. Our deliverance from these sensual sins of the flesh will come through walking in love, even as Christ also loved us. Victory will come when we deny ourselves and take up the cross to follow Jesus daily (Luke 9:23). When we purpose in our heart to please God and the Heavenly Father, when we purpose in our heart to be what He wants us to be, we will not follow the selfish desires of the flesh.

We are saved by grace––grace alone; but the man

who deliberately uses grace as an excuse to follow the lust of the flesh is disillusioned and has been deceived with vain words delivered by a vain preacher. It is true that we are not saved by abstaining from fornication, adultery and filthiness (we can abstain from these things and still be lost); but the grace of God teaches us to deny these things (Titus 2:11—15).

In Romans 8:4 the Spirit teaches us that the righteousness of the Law is fulfilled in us who walk not after the flesh but after the Spirit. As I have tried to point out, the Spirit leads us into paths of right living——*to the glory of God*, not that we might boast, brag, or display our holiness. We live holy through the leadership of the Holy Spirit, to the glory of a holy God. The person who declares himself to be in grace and yet follows the lust of the flesh, never displaying works of righteousness, should read again these words: "But wilt thou know, O VAIN MAN, that faith without works is dead?" (James 2:20).

To young Timothy, Paul said: "Nevertheless, THE FOUNDATION OF GOD STANDETH SURE, having this seal, The Lord knoweth them that are His. And, Let every one that nameth the name of Christ depart from iniquity" (II Tim. 2:19). If we do not depart from unrighteousness, then by our daily living we testify that we are not the children of love, but that we are still the children of wrath (Eph. 2:1—3). We are the children of disobedience if we have not obeyed from the heart that form of doctrine mentioned in Romans 6 . . . the form of doctrine that causes us to yield our members as instruments of righteousness unto God.

Verse 7 is clear and needs no comment: "Be not ye therefore partakers with them." We are to have no fellowship with the unfruitful works of darkness; we are rather to reprove them. We are to walk in the light, not as children of night.

WE ARE THE CHILDREN OF LIGHT

Verses 8—17: "For ye were sometimes darkness, but now are ye light in the Lord: walk as children of light: (For the fruit of the Spirit is in all goodness and righteousness and truth;) Proving what is acceptable unto the Lord. And have no fellowship with the unfruitful works of darkness, but rather reprove them. For it is a shame even to speak of those things which are done of them in secret. But all things that are reproved are made manifest by the light: for whatsoever doth make manifest is light. Wherefore he saith, Awake thou that sleepest, and arise from the dead, and Christ shall give thee light. See then that ye walk circumspectly, not as fools, but as wise, redeeming the time, because the days are evil. Wherefore be ye not unwise, but understanding what the will of the Lord is."

According to these words dictated by the Holy Spirit and penned down by the Apostle Paul, it is utterly impossible for any person to be saved and not know it. Sinners are darkness . . . they are blacked out, they are in the dark. When we are saved we are transformed out of darkness into light. To be converted from sin to salvation is just like walking out of a dark room into a room where a thousand-watt bulb is blazing light. It is impossible to shut your eyes and open them and not know the difference, if you are in the sunlight of the noonday. You can close your eyes, and it becomes dark; you open your eyes and it is light. Sinners are in darkness . . . Christians are in light. When the Spirit comes in, we become the children of light, we walk in the light. The Spirit proves the things that are acceptable unto God.

Verse 11 is not a suggestion——it is a positive and

direct command: "HAVE NO FELLOWSHIP WITH THE UNFRUITFUL WORKS OF DARKNESS, BUT RATHER REPROVE THEM." We are not to fellowship with the enemies of Jesus Christ. Born again Christians are not to fellowship with the lust of the flesh and the ungodliness of the world. Friendship with the world is spiritual adultery against God. We are not to fellowship with liberals, modernists and haters of God, deniers of the faith.

It is not enough to stay away from them——but we are to "REPROVE THEM." As a minister of the Gospel, it is not enough for me to abstain from the appearance of evil——I must speak out against it. It is not enough that I stay out of bars, nightclubs and dancehalls, it is not enough that I refuse to embrace liberalism and modernism and stay away from them; but as a minister of the Gospel I must reprove them, I must speak out against them and warn people. I would not be at all surprised if through these lines I am not speaking to someone who is truly born again and yet you are supporting a liberal or modernist . . . a man who uses some of the modern translations of the Bible which soft-pedal the virgin birth, deny the blood, declare the Fatherhood of God and the brotherhood of man. You should not support any person unless he declares the truth and the doctrine of Christ . . . and if you do support such a person you are guilty of his evil deeds. Read II John and you will see clearly that you are not to invite a liberal, modernist, false religionist or member of a cult into your home. If you do invite them into your house and bid them Godspeed you are guilty of aiding and comforting the enemies of Jesus Christ. *"Have no fellowship with the unfruitful works of darkness"* is a command . . . it is not a suggestion! It is shameful to even talk about the things that are "done in secret"——the sensual sins of the flesh.

All things that are reproved are made manifest by

the light. In other words, if we are born again, the Holy Ghost will show us the things that are right and the things that are wrong. He will lead us into the paths of right-eousness, He will lead us around the cesspools and pit-falls of the lust of sin and the world. If we walk in the light we will not fulfill the desires of the flesh and of the mind. We must be led by the Spirit or we cannot over-come the world. Paul cries out in verse 14, "Awake, thou that sleepest!" We need to be alert, we need to be sober and vigilant. Our adversary, the devil, as a roaring lion is walking about, seeking whom he may devour, and he is no respecter of persons——never forget that! Read and study I Peter 5:8–10.

We are to see to it that we walk circumspectly. We are not to walk as fools. We are wise because we have the Spirit and the wisdom of God . . . Christ is made unto us wisdom (I Cor. 1:29–30). We are not to waste time . . . it is a sin to waste time. The days are evil, we are members of the body of Christ, and we are commanded to preach the Gospel to every creature . . . to carry the good news of the Gospel to those who are lost. To waste time is to sin. We are to buy up the opportunities that present themselves and tell out the Good News daily to those who need to be saved.

From verse 17 we know that the unwise do not seek God's will——but we who have wisdom and understanding are to seek His will and follow in His steps. In John 17 He declared that He came here to follow the bidding of the Father and to do the Father's will. He said, "Not my will, but thine be done." Just before He gave up His life on the cross He said, "It is finished!" We should at all times seek God's will in everything.

Believer, never do anything or go anywhere if you are not sure in your mind that it is right. Anything that is

178

doubtful is sinful——because the Holy Spirit would not put a question mark in your mind if it were right. "Whatsoever is not of faith is sin"——and certainly faith knows no doubt. If there is a question mark around the places you go, the things you do, the songs you sing, the company you keep, the language you use, you may rest assured it is not God's will for you to do those things. Submit your will to God, and let Him have His way through the leadership of the Holy Spirit in your life.

ANOTHER COMMANDMENT TO BELIEVERS

Verses 18–21: "And be not drunk with wine, wherein is excess; but be filled with the Spirit; Speaking to yourselves in psalms and hymns and spiritual songs, singing and making melody in your heart to the Lord; giving thanks always for all things unto God and the Father in the name of our Lord Jesus Christ; submitting yourselves one to another in the fear of God."

Again let me point out that verse 18 is not a suggestion. The Holy Spirit did not say, "If it is convenient, be filled with the Spirit," or "If you think it best, be filled with the Spirit," or, "If your circumstances permit, be filled with the Spirit."

There is a negative and a positive:

1. (Negative): *"Be not drunk with wine."* Dear reader, do you believe it is a sin to be drunk with wine? Would you get drunk on wine? What would you think of a minister or a professed Christian who gets drunk on wine? Would you say they are living right? ———???

2. (Positive): "BUT BE FILLED WITH THE SPIRIT." If it is wrong to be drunk with wine, it is also wrong NOT to be filled with the Spirit. Do not get drunk on wine——but be filled with the Holy Spirit.

179

Beloved, this does not say, "Be baptized with the Holy Ghost." The believer is *already baptized* into the body of Christ by the Holy Spirit (I Cor. 12:12-13). This is altogether another truth. As I have stated several times in these messages, it is altogether possible to be born of the Spirit, indwelt by the Spirit, baptized into the body of Christ by the Spirit, and still not be *filled* with the Spirit. This is not a second work of grace . . . it is a full surrender of soul, mind and body—the body which is the temple of the Holy Ghost. Paul said to the Romans, "I beseech you to present your bodies a living sacrifice, which is your reasonable service." It is reasonable to yield soul, spirit and body. It is reasonable to be filled with the Holy Spirit; and it is not right—it is sinful— NOT to be filled.

To be filled with the Spirit, we must be emptied of all the things named in the preceding verses of chapters four and five . . . the things of the flesh, the things of the natural man. If we are to be a spiritual man, full grown to maturity, filled with the Spirit, we must first be emptied. You cannot fill a container with water until it is first emptied of everything else. If there are three grains of sand in a glass, you cannot fill that glass with water—it will be *water and sand* until the sand is removed. A believer cannot be filled with the Holy Spirit until that believer permits the Lord Jesus to empty his heart of everything of the world, the flesh, and the devil. When the heart is emptied, then the Holy Spirit can and will fill that individual.

In verse 19 we have the *evidence* of the filling of the Spirit:

1. We speak to ourselves in psalms, hymns, and spiritual songs. We sing, and make melody in our heart to the Lord. Please do not be offended or angry . . . please

take this in the spirit in which I am giving it: A person who is filled with the Spirit does not have to advertise his filling of the Spirit to his fellowman. He does not go to church, and brag and boast concerning his holiness and his purity, his godliness and his spirituality. A person who is filled with the Spirit sings psalms, songs, and makes melody in the heart TO THE LORD. The Holy Spirit is in the world to glorify Jesus . . . He is not in the world to glorify *us*, nor to glorify us before men. The person who is possessed by and filled entirely with the Holy Spirit will make melody unto the Lord——not unto man! A spiritually minded person never advertises his holiness. His daily living advertises his righteousness of heart. People know by his daily practices of life.

2. A Spirit-filled person is a thankful person . . . always, for all things. He is thankful to God the Father in the name of Jesus, because it is in Jesus that the filling of the Spirit is possible. If Jesus had not been willing to do the Father's will, if He had not left the Father's bosom and surrendered Himself into the hands of wicked men who nailed Him to the cross, if He had not died, we could not enjoy this precious salvation and the glorious filling of the Holy Spirit. A Spirit-filled person will be always thanking God for the Lord Jesus, and for the spiritual joy, peace, blessings, assurance and security that we have through the shed blood and the grace of God *in* the Lord Jesus. A Spirit-filled life is a life that makes melody in the heart to the Lord, and gives thanks to God for the Lord Jesus. Are you filled with the Spirit? Do you know the fulness of the Spirit? It is your blessing to possess if you are willing to pay the price. Redemption is free——you cannot pay the price for redemption. Salvation is free . . . but there is a price to be paid if we enjoy the fulness of the Spirit. The price is to submit to God to be emptied of self, selfishness,

sensual lust, and the world; and when you are emptied, you are then ready to be filled. "Be not drunk with wine ——but be filled with the Spirit!"

In verse 21 we are commanded to submit one to another in the fear of God. One of the greatest needs in the local church today is for people to fear God, and work in harmony and unity. One of the terrible sins in the visible church today is the lack of unity. As in the Corinthian church, every person has a song, every person has a doctrine, every person has a testimony, every person has a sermon——and everybody wants to run things. God has an abundance of bosses, superintendents, presidents, chairmen of the board; He is looking for common laborers . . . folks who will get down in the dirt and be a humble servant. We are to submit one to another, and when we are filled with the Spirit we do that. We do not feel our importance, and we esteem our brethren higher and nobler than ourselves.

I would heartily agree that there are few examples of a Spirit-filled life today——but thank God, there are some. God help you and me to permit the Holy Spirit to search our hearts, God help us to be emptied of everything that would hinder the cause of Christ, the building up of the Body, the bringing in of the unsaved. God help us to be filled with the Spirit.

A CLEAR ILLUSTRATION OF WHAT THE CHURCH IS

Verses 22–33: "Wives, submit yourselves unto your own husbands, as unto the Lord. For the husband is the head of the wife, even as Christ is the head of the church: and He is the saviour of the body. Therefore as the church is subject unto Christ, so let the wives be to their own husbands in every thing. Husbands, love your wives, even as Christ also loved the church, and gave Himself for it; that He might sanctify and cleanse it with the washing of water by the Word, That He might present it to Himself a glorious church, not having spot, or wrinkle, or any such thing; but that it would be holy and without blemish. So ought men to love their wives as their own bodies. He that loveth his wife loveth himself. For no man ever yet hated his own flesh; but nourisheth and cherisheth it, even as the Lord the church: For we are members of His body, of His flesh, and of His bones. For this cause shall a man leave his father and mother, and shall be joined unto his wife, and they two shall be one flesh. This is a great mystery: but I speak concerning Christ and the church. Nevertheless let every one of you in particular so love his wife even as himself; and the wife see that she reverence her husband."

The truth set forth here is unmistakable, crystal clear, easily understood by those who are willing to accept the Word of God and compare spiritual things with spiritual. If you have no preconceived ideas, if you are not following man-made dogma and doctrine, you can clearly see tremendous truths laid down in our present verses.

Here the Holy Spirit uses the husband and the wife to show the spiritual picture of the New Testament church. He clearly states that wives are to be subject to their own husbands. They are to submit to their own husbands as unto the Lord. (Of course, this is in the true spiritual sense. A born again woman is not to submit to sin in order to please her husband—she is supposed to please the Lord. It is perfectly legitimate and right for a woman to go as far as she possibly can to please an unsaved husband—but she is not supposed to deny the Lord.) If the husband is saved, the husband is the head of that wife.

Paul illustrates by saying, "For the husband is the

head of the wife, EVEN AS CHRIST IS THE HEAD OF THE CHURCH." This is clear and unmistakable. Christ is the head of the church . . . not the Apostle Peter nor the Pope of Rome. The Pope of Rome is the head of the Roman Catholic church, to be sure; but Jesus Christ is the head of the church of God. The Bible clearly and unmistakably states that Christ is the head of the church; therefore, no man or woman is, has ever been, nor ever will be, head of the church. Jesus is the head; He is also the foundation (I Cor. 3:11). But Paul goes further:

The husband is to protect the wife because she is the weaker vessel. The woman was made from a rib, removed from beneath Adam's arm. The woman should be under the protection of the husband, who is the stronger and who is the head. Jesus in like manner is the head of the church, and He is the Saviour of the body. He protects the body, thank God. As I have tried to point out, we are not saved and left to fight our battles alone. We have within us the Holy Spirit . . . a greater power than the spirit of Satan (I John 4:4, Rom. 8:35–39). Jesus is not only the *head* of the church, but He also *protects* the church; and one day it will be presented to Him by God the Father, without spot or wrinkle . . . there will not be one iota of sin in the church when it is presented to the Lord Jesus Christ.

In verse 24, Paul goes a step further: Jesus is the head of the church, He is the Saviour of the church—— therefore, *the church is subject to Jesus.* No two-legged human being on the face of this earth has any right to change anything in the Word of God pertaining to the church of God. Jesus said, "Nicodemus, you must be born of the Spirit"——and it is still, "Ye must be born of the Spirit." We must be saved by grace through faith. The entrance into the church is by salvation (Acts 2:47) and if you are not saved you are not a member of the New

Testament church. Jesus is the Saviour; the church is subject to Him.

Paul goes a step further in the natural realm, and admonishes wives to be subject to their own husbands in everything. Paul is thinking in terms of believers——not sinners. The wife is to be subject to a Godly husband because the husband is head of the wife. The church is to be subject to Jesus——not to a preacher, a board of deacons or trustees, not a bishop. No man has any right to dictate to the Lord's church, nor make changes in it. It is finished. "Thy Word is forever settled in heaven." Not one jot or tittle will ever pass away. The church is subject to the doctrine of Jesus Christ, not to the dogmas and traditions of men. Regardless of what changes are made in doctrines and in the rules and regulations of the church, you can mark it well that the rules, regulations, doctrines of truth having to do with the church, are today as they were when Jesus said, "Upon this rock I will build my church!" The warning is the same: "If any come to you and bring not this doctrine, do not invite him into your house and do not bid him God speed" (II John).

In verse 25, Paul goes further: The husband is head of the wife——but *he is not the boss.* He is to love his wife as Jesus loved the church and gave Himself for it. That gives a little different light on the relationship between a Christian man and Christian woman. A believing husband is not to dominate, dictate, and domineer the woman. He is to love that woman, lead and protect her; and if she is the kind of woman she ought to be, she wants to be loved, led and protected by the husband. A woman who has the right spirit does not desire to boss a man.

Verse 26 is very enlightening: "That He (Jesus) might sanctify and cleanse it (the church)" . . . but how? "By the washing . . . ." What washing? The baptistry?

185

Baptism? The river Jordan? The One to whom we are subject gives the answer: ". . . BY THE WASHING OF THE WATER BY THE WORD." There is not enough water in the river Jordan and in all the baptistries in all the world to wash away the least sin you have ever committed. Water baptism has nothing to do with redemption. Water baptism has nothing to do with salvation. Water baptism is an ordinance of the New Testament church, which testifies that the person being baptized has died to the world, died to sin, is buried with Christ, and is raised to walk in newness of life. Water baptism does not wash away sins. The water referred to in John 3:5 and the water that cleanses the church is the Word of God. For instance: "NOW YE ARE CLEAN THROUGH THE WORD WHICH I HAVE SPOKEN UNTO YOU" (John 15:3). Jesus sat by Jacob's well. A woman came . . . a woman who had been married five times, and who had a husband to whom she was not married. Jesus said, "Give me a drink." She said, "I do not understand it. The Jews hate the Samaritans, and yet, you (a Jew), ask me (a Samaritan), for a drink." Jesus said, "If you knew the gift of God, you would be asking *me* for a drink." The woman said, "I want this water . . . ." During the conversation the woman said, "I know that Messiah cometh, and when He comes He will tell us all things." Jesus gave her the water. Do you know what He gave her? He said, "I that speak to thee am He!" And when she heard those words she threw down her waterpots and ran to town with an artesian well bubbling over in her soul. The words that Jesus gave her, from the first word to the last one He spoke, brought living water. The Word IS the water . . . living water; and the Word brings salvation. The Word cleanses from all sin. The Word sanctifies: "Sanctify them through thy Word. Thy Word is truth" (John 17:17). The Word cleanses (John 15:3). The Word is the seed that brings the new birth (I Peter 1:23). Bap-

186

tism is not the water referred to here—nor any other place having to do with cleansing from the filthiness of sin.

In verse 27, the church will be presented to Christ . . . a glorious church, a spotless church, a holy church, a church without wrinkle or blemish; blazing white holiness, purity, righteousness, godliness will be on display when the church is presented to Jesus at the marriage supper in the sky. What a picture! What a tremendous truth. What a glorious fact. I am so glad I am a member of that body! And dear reader, if you are not a member of that body, you can be right now, this moment, if you will bow your head, close your eyes, and put your trust in Jesus. He will save you.

In verse 28, Paul goes further with his illustration. Men ought to love their wives as their own body. A man should protect his wife just like he would protect himself. He should love his wife like he loves himself. A man and wife are *one*. People who are married in the Lord are not two people—they are one flesh. They love alike, they live alike, they think alike. They rejoice together, weep together. That is the way Christian marriage ought to be—and if *God* joined more people together the divorce courts would be out of business! No man hates his own flesh. We feed our flesh, we cherish our flesh . . . and we look after ourselves. We should do the same for our wife.

In the last part of verse 29 we read, ". . . EVEN AS THE LORD THE CHURCH." The Lord Jesus is looking after His church, praise God! He looks after His little children. I am glad the Lord is my Shepherd. He leadeth me beside the still waters, He restoreth my soul, He leadeth me in the paths of righteousness, He prepares a table before me in the presence of mine enemies, He anointeth my head with oil . . . He makes my cup to run over, and He will give me goodness and mercy all the days of my life and then He will give me a place in the Father's house forever. Hallelujah! What a Saviour! What a Shepherd!

Why does Jesus do all this for us? Verse 30 answers: We born again children of God are members of His body. Think of it! We are united to His body. In the spiritual aspect we are NOW members of His body. We are NOW members of His flesh and of His bones. Those of us who are born again believers did not join the New Testament church by filling out a card. We became part of the body of Christ by faith in His blood. The Holy Spirit united us, welded us, put us into the body. No wonder He looks after us! *You*, father or mother, look after *your* little children if you are the kind of mom and dad you ought to be. Jesus is the kind of Saviour He ought to be, and He looks after His own. Praise His name!

Love:

No word in any language so fully embodies the Gospel of the Grace of God, no word so adequately represents Christ and what He did to bring about our salvation, as does *love*. What a standard God has set up concerning the love between a man and his wife: *"As Christ loved the church!"* Certainly the love of Christ for the church is past finding out, it knows no boundaries, it knows no barriers. Christ's love is unspeakable, indescribable, unknowable in its fulness. In the eternity behind us He loved us, He gave Himself for us, even while we were yet dead in trespasses and sins . . . while we were yet ungodly. At this present hour He loves us and is sanctifying and cleansing believers (members of the church) with the washing of the water by the Word. But that is not all: Out yonder in the future, because of His great love wherewith He loved us, He will present the church to Himself, "a glorious church not having spot or wrinkle or any such thing." What love!

The reason so clearly set forth here, that men should love their wives as they love their own bodies, is simply because a man's wife IS his own body. "He that loveth his wife loveth himself." The story is clearly set forth in Genesis 2:21—23: "And the Lord caused a deep sleep to fall upon Adam, and he slept: and He took one of his ribs, and closed up the flesh instead thereof; and the rib, which the Lord God had taken from man, made He a woman, and brought her unto the man. And Adam said, This is now BONE OF MY BONES, AND FLESH OF MY FLESH: she shall be called Woman, because she was taken out of Man."

We have here the divine basis for marriage. From this divine basis for marriage comes the mutual obligation between husband and wife. The wife is the body of the husband——a position of submission; but the wife is also "his own flesh." Let the husband love the wife with the same love wherewith he loves himself, because she is his own flesh. God created man out of dust——but woman was taken out of man. She is bone of man's bone, and flesh of man's flesh.

So it is with the church: Adam's sleep was a type of the death of Jesus Christ (the second Adam). The Lord Jesus' side was opened, too . . . after He was dead the soldier pierced His side (John 19:34) and there came out both blood and water. God caused a deep sleep to fall upon Adam, and from his side was taken the rib from which God formed woman; God put a deep sleep on the second Adam, *His* side was opened . . . and through the opening of that side another body is being formed . . . HIS body, the church. He is the head, we are members of His body, and the only way we can become a member of that body is to accept His pierced side . . . the shed blood.

Therefore, New Testament marriage is an intimate INDISSOLUBLE UNION. When a man and woman are joined together in marriage by the Lord, they become one flesh . . . they are no longer two. "Therefore shall a man leave his father and his mother, and shall cleave unto his wife" (Gen. 2:24). In the same way, the Son of God has a Bride. He left the Father's house, came into the world, died on the cross, His side was opened––and through His shed blood we who believe become members of His body, His Bride, and one day we will be presented to Him without spot or wrinkle. "This is a great mystery: but I speak concerning Christ and the church."

Dear friend, would it be possible for the Lord Jesus to cast off the church? Would it be possible for Jesus to divorce the church and set it aside? I ask you then in the same sensible line of reasoning, if man and woman become one flesh when they are united by Almighty God in holy marriage and divinely instituted matrimony, can a man actually sever relationship with his wife? Or can the wife sever relationship with her husband? The marriage bonds cannot be broken if they are in the Lord. They are of kindred nature, and man and woman become one flesh. Love and reverence cause men and women to become one in marriage. True marriage is a sanctified experience––the husband is dedicated to the wife, the wife is dedicated to the husband, the relationship is sacred and sweet; and when God joins two together they can never be put asunder by men or demons because they are no longer two––they are one.

God frowns on many marriages in this day and hour ––quick marriages, marriages that are no more than a civil or legal ceremony to put two parties together, to live together in pleasure and sin for a season and then separate and go through the same mockery again. You must not forget, beloved, that marriages are made in heaven. Marriages that are in the Lord are sacred and holy, and they have a tremendous spiritual setting . . . they are a type of the New Testament church. God provided the first bride, God performed the first marriage—and God instructed man that he is to leave and forsake everything else . . . but is never to forsake his wife. Man is the head of the woman, and therefore he should be the leader in all things, especially in spiritual matters. God have mercy on lawyers and judges who break up homes in the divorce courts and make orphans out of little children who bear the image of parents they did not choose . . . bone of their bone and flesh of their flesh. Such parents bring children into the world—and then separate, leaving the children with the stigma of being the child of a divorcee. To the young and to the unwed, let me advise that you not marry until you know beyond the shadow of a doubt that God is in the union. You may think it is terrible if you are in your early or late twenties and not married; but do not forget, it is much, much better to be a single girl than to be a heartbroken wife, married to the wrong man! It is much better to remain single than to marry and then have that marriage end in a divorce court. But thank God, in the spiritual sense, when we believe on the Lord Jesus Christ, God does join us to the body of the Lord Jesus, we become one flesh—and praise God, all hell and earth cannot separate us from the body of Christ.

Chapter five closes with the clear, understandable statement, "NEVERTHELESS let every one of you in particular so love his wife even as himself; and the wife see that she reverence her husband." Certainly when the husband loves the wife as he loves himself, and when the wife has reverence for such a loving husband, all hell could not separate them nor tear them apart. That is exactly as the Lord Jesus would have it.

1. Children, obey your parents in the Lord: for this is right.

2. Honour thy father and mother; which is the first commandment with promise;

3. That it may be well with thee, and thou mayest live long on the earth.

4. And, ye fathers, provoke not your children to wrath: but bring them up in the nurture and admonition of the Lord.

5. Servants, be obedient to them that are your masters according to the flesh, with fear and trembling, in singleness of your heart, as unto Christ;

6. Not with eyeservice, as menpleasers; but as the servants of Christ, doing the will of God from the heart;

7. With good will doing service, as to the Lord, and not to men:

8. Knowing that whatsoever good thing any man doeth, the same shall he receive of the Lord, whether he be bond or free.

9. And, ye masters, do the same things unto them, forbearing threatening: knowing that your Master also is in heaven; neither is there respect of persons with him.

10. Finally, my brethren, be strong in the Lord, and in the power of his might.

11. Put on the whole armour of God, that ye may be able to stand against the wiles of the devil.

12. For we wrestle not against flesh and blood, but against principalities, against powers, against the rulers of the darkness of this world, against spiritual wickedness in high places.

13. Wherefore take unto you the whole armour of God, that ye may be able to withstand in the evil day, and having done all, to stand.

14. Stand therefore, having your loins girt about with truth, and having on the breastplate of righteousness;

15. And your feet shod with the preparation of the gospel of peace;

16. Above all, taking the shield of faith, wherewith ye shall be able to quench all the fiery darts of the wicked.

17. And take the helmet of salvation, and the sword of the Spirit, which is the word of God:

18. Praying always with all prayer and supplication in the Spirit, and watching thereunto with all perseverance and supplication for all saints;

19. And for me, that utterance may be given unto me, that I may open my mouth boldly, to make known the mystery of the gospel,

20. For which I am an ambassador in bonds: that therein I may speak boldly, as I ought to speak.

21. But that ye also may know my affairs, and how I do, Tychicus, a beloved brother and faithful minister in the Lord, shall make known to you all things:

22. Whom I have sent unto you for the same purpose, that ye might know our affairs, and that he might comfort your hearts.

23. Peace be to the brethren, and love with faith, from God the Father and the Lord Jesus Christ.

24. Grace be with all them that love our Lord Jesus Christ in sincerity. Amen.

SPIRIT FILLED BELIEVERS –
THEIR CHILDREN – THEIR SERVANTS

Verses 1–3: "Children, obey your parents in the Lord: for this is right. Honour thy father and mother; which is the first commandment with promise; that it may be well with thee, and thou mayest live long on the earth."

The admonition of these verses is needed today as in no other age since Adam. Never in history have children been so disobedient and disrespectful to parents as in this present day. God knows the end from the beginning, and He knew the command given in our present Scripture would be needed in this twentieth century.

Some will not accept what I am going to say: Children are to obey their parents *in the Lord*. Children are to honor their father and their mother until such honoring of parents brings DIShonor upon the God who loved the world enough to permit Jesus to die for all sinners.

There are many children who love the Lord, but whose parents do not. The children have been born again, the parents have not. They drink, they gamble, they swear. To those saved children I would say, You honor your parents as far as it is possible without dishonoring God. Do not be ugly or hateful . . . as a Christian you should not act unseemly. Honor and obey your parents until you reach the place where you must commit sin against God in order to obey them——and then you are not duty bound to do so. It may cost you your home, it may cost you your education, it may cost you your part in your parents' will . . . you may be left out of the inheritance. But it would be far better to be left out of an earthly father's estate than to miss heaven! There is nothing on this earth worth going to hell for. So . . . children, obey your parents *in the Lord.* If your parents are godly, you obey them. Do not question their commands, their advice, or their wishes. If your parents are born again, you obey them. Walk in the path laid down by your parents concerning your friends, the places you go, the company you keep. Parents who love the Lord will not lead you astray.

Honoring father and mother in the Lord has a promise along with it. I am sure I will die at an early age if Jesus tarries. I will not live to be an old man. From the time I was nine years old until I was nineteen, I did not honor and respect my parents. I broke my father's heart. I put him in an early grave. I robbed him of his money and of his wealth. I dishonored him to the extent that I brought reproach and disgrace upon his name. I was known as the black sheep of the Greene family. Because of my wretched living, I was not welcome in some homes where other young people were.*

Since I did not honor my parents, I lost the promise of long life upon this earth. You children who have no respect for your Christian parents, who are breaking their hearts by the things you do, the places you go, the company you keep, *mark it well:* You will not live to a ripe old age, because honoring godly parents promises long life and blessings on the earth. If you are deliberately disobeying godly parents, rest assured that you will reap what you are sowing!

Verse 4: "And, ye fathers, provoke not your children

*Order the life story of Evangelist Greene, entitled "From Disgrace to Grace." Send $1.00 for radio expense. The book will be sent to you postpaid.

to wrath: but bring them up in the nurture and admonition of the Lord."

We hear much today about juvenile delinquency. I readily confess that we do have much delinquency among juveniles——but I hasten to say that in many cases the fault is not with the child, but with the parents. I know some parents have done their very best by their children ——and even then the children have gone the way of the world; but in most cases the teenagers who drink, curse, smoke, lie and steal have been brought up in homes where they were not chastened or controlled.

The Bible promises, "Train up a child in the way it should go, and when it is old it will not depart." The Word of God goes further to say, "He that spareth the rod hateth his son." Today many children are juvenile delinquents because they were not brought up in the nurture and admonition of the Lord. The time to begin training a child is not when the child is three, four, or five years old . . . but when it is three, four, or five *days* old. Some parents wonder why they cannot control their children. The answer is simple: They did not begin in time! The majority of children will do almost anything they can get away with. You must remember that your child was born in a tabernacle of sin . . . totally depraved . . . and it is just as natural for a child to resist authority and go the way of the flesh, as it is for the sun to rise in the east. The inclination to do wrong is born in a child. The child must be taught to do right.

Do not misunderstand me: If a baby dies, the grace of God takes care of the innocent. I do not know any definite age of accountability——the Bible does not tell us. Some children become responsible at a much earlier age than others. There is no set age when children can be saved . . . but long before they are old enough to know they are sinners, they demonstrate the spirit of a sinner. They scream, they fight, and they have all of the marks of their depravity. Therefore, the time to begin training the child is in the crib. If your children do not respect you, if they do not say "Yes, ma'am," and "Yes, sir," it is your fault! When you tell your child to do something, if he replies with "I will not do it," or "I will do it when I get ready," do not blame the child . . . blame yourself. Parents are responsible for the child they brought into this world.

"Ye fathers, provoke not your children to wrath." In using the word "fathers" there is no thought of taking responsibility from the mother. The word "father" is a term for parenthood, and is doubtless designed to remind us that we stand to our children as our Heavenly Father does to us. The parents' duty is stated negatively and positively:

1. NOT to incite to anger by severity of treatment that arouses resentment and robs the child of respect for parental authority when not exercised with restraint.

2. *Rather* to nurture them, to do everything that is conducive to their growth and development in the continuous process of child-training . . . for such is the meaning of the words *educate, culture, discipline.*

When a child is young the mind is being molded, and we can bend that tender twig to shape it into a beautiful life if we handle it right. But if we anger the child by tantalizing it, or making a public example of it, storming out at the child in public, we are doing wrong.

A parent should never whip or chasten a child while angry. If your child does something that causes you to become angry, you should wait until the anger subsides, until you are calm, and then chasten the child. May I add that there is an age when whipping will no longer help a child. What that age is will differ in children. Some children will bear chastening much longer than others——but as a parent you can know when the child is too old, too big, to be chastened with a switch or a leather strap. When that happens, there are other ways of correcting, such as taking away some of the privileges or something they particularly love, which will do more good than whipping. Reason with the child, and try through understanding and reason to show him that the correction is for his own good.

Parents should train their children in the things of the Lord. The Bible should be read in their presence, prayer should be carried on in their presence, grace should be said at the table always and at every meal. The children should not be *sent* to Sunday school and church—— they should be *taken* to Sunday school and church by their parents. If we bring up our children in the nurture and admonition of the Lord the Lord will certainly keep His part of the bargain . . . "Train up a child in the way it should go, and when it is old it will not depart."

Positively, we are to nurture our children in the things of the Lord. In the Old Testament, the Jewish homemaker followed this godly advice: "And these words, which I command thee this day, shall be in thine heart: and thou shalt teach them diligently unto thy children, and shalt talk of them when thou sittest in thine house, and when thou walkest by the way, and when thou liest down, and when thou risest up. And thou shalt bind them for a sign upon thine hand, and they shall be as frontlets between thine eyes. And thou shalt write them upon the posts of thy house, and on thy gates" (Deut. 6:6–9).

That is Old Testament gospel——but it is also good, sound, divine advice. It takes great churches to make a great nation. It takes great homes to make great churches.

The break-down of the home is one of the main points of Communism . . . the tearing down of family life. Whether or not you recognize it, whether or not you will admit it, the home in America is becoming a place to dress and undress, a place from which we make our appointments and dress to meet them. Everything in the modern home is controlled by a switch . . . except the children! The switch that used to stand in the corner, the switch that was the making of men like Abraham Lincoln, George Washington and others, has been taken out . . . it is in use no more. God have mercy on the children of this hour. Old-fashioned mothers and fathers, old-fashioned home training, and old-fashioned discipline would answer the question, "What can we do about juvenile delinquency?" Let me repeat: The blame for juvenile delinquency does not lie at the feet of the children . . . it lies at the doorsteps of the parents who are responsible for bringing those children into the world. The children had no choice, they did not choose their parents, they did not choose to come into this world. Therefore, the parents responsible for the children being here owe them a tremendous debt. If we do not fulfill our obligation to our children, we will pay for it in the heartbreak of the child, and we will continue to pay in eternity!

Verses 5—9: "Servants, be obedient to them that are your masters according to the flesh, with fear and trembling, in singleness of your heart, as unto Christ; not with eyeservice, as menpleasers; but as the servants of Christ, doing the will of God from the heart; with good will doing service, as to the Lord, and not to men: Knowing that whatsoever good thing any man doeth, the same shall he receive of the Lord, whether he be bond or free. And, ye masters, do the same things unto them, forbearing threatening: knowing that your Master also is in heaven; neither is there respect of persons with Him."

In these verses we learn the duty of servants to their masters. Servants are to be obedient to their masters. In Bible lands, servants were counted part of the household, and yet they were what we would call "slaves." The Greek word used for servant throughout the New Testament could have been translated into the English word "slave." Some have suggested that since this is true, Christianity puts its approval upon slavery——but quite the opposite is true: The teaching in our present verses lifts the servant OUT of slavery, and sets him free with a freedom never known to a slave. Verse 9 closes with the statement, "NEITHER IS THERE RESPECT OF PERSONS WITH HIM." The servant is to obey his master.

The motive of service is what counts with the Lord . . . not the external show. In the sermon on the mount, Jesus condemned externalism in religion. "Take heed that ye do not your alms before men, to be seen of them: otherwise ye have no reward of your Father which is in heaven. THEREFORE, when thou doest thine alms, do not sound a trumpet before thee, as the hypocrites do in the synagogues and in the streets, that they may have glory of men. Verily I say unto you, *They have their reward*. But when thou doest alms, let not thy left hand know what thy right hand doeth; that thine alms may be in secret: and thy Father which seeth in secret HIMSELF SHALL REWARD THEE OPENLY. And when thou prayest, thou shalt not be as the hypocrites are: for they love to pray standing in the synagogues and in the corners of the streets, that they may be seen of men. Verily I say unto you, *They have their reward*. But thou, when thou prayest, enter into thy closet, and when thou hast shut thy door, pray to thy Father which is in secret; and thy Father which seeth in secret SHALL REWARD THEE OPENLY. But when ye pray, use not vain repetitions, as the heathen do: for they think that they shall be heard for their much speaking. . . . Moreover when ye fast, be not as the hypocrites, of a sad countenance: for they disfigure their faces, that they may appear unto men to fast. Verily I say unto you, *They have their reward*. But thou, when thou fastest, anoint thine head, and wash thy face; that thou appear not unto men to fast, but unto thy Father which is in secret: and thy Father, which seeth in secret, SHALL REWARD THEE OPENLY. Lay not up for yourselves treasures upon earth, where moth and rust doth corrupt, and where thieves break through and steal: But lay up for yourselves treasures in heaven, where neither moth nor rust doth corrupt, and where thieves do not break through nor steal: FOR WHERE YOUR TREASURE IS, THERE WILL YOUR HEART BE ALSO" (Matt. 6:1–7, 16–21).

In these verses, Jesus clearly teaches that whatsoever we do we should do to the glory of God . . . we should not do it to be seen of men, but "AS UNTO THE LORD," and if we do what we do as unto the Lord, He who sees in secret will reward us in full, openly, "at that day." Paul said, "For I know whom I have believed, and am persuaded that He is able to keep that which I have committed unto Him *against that day*" (II Tim. 1:12b).

I am glad that whatsoever we commit unto the Lord Jesus, He is very capable and able to protect and keep for us until "that day" when we stand before Him to receive our just reward. Servants, give your masters good measure . . . heaped up, pressed down, running over. Do it as unto the Lord——not to please men, but because you are a son of God.

To those of you who are masters, let me give warning: Do not be a slave driver. Do not be lords over God's heritage. Do not be overbearing and threatening, because you, too, have a Master——even the Lord of heaven——and one day you will stand before Him. I am sure you want your Master to deal with you in mercy, love and kindness—but remember, as we sow—we reap!

If the employers and employees would practice the Gospel truth laid down here by Paul, the labor troubles and unrest throughout America would cease to be. Thank God, during the reign of the Lord Jesus there will be no labor trouble—nor any other trouble—because the knowledge of the Lord will cover the earth as the waters now cover the sea. A baptism of God's love from heaven is what is needed by labor and management. Then the masters would love their servants, and the servants would love their masters . . . and *love covers every need of the human race.*

In Proverbs 10:12 we read, "Love covereth all sins." In I Peter 4:8 we read, "Love covereth a multitude of sins." In I Corinthians 13:7 we read, "Love covers all things." God's love in Christ Jesus—who came not to be ministered unto but to minister, not to be served but to serve—has provided for us redemption and the right to a home in heaven. Only through the love of God could such provision have been made. The love of God in Christ Jesus forgives and forgets our sin and ungodliness— but *only in the blood.* "When I see the blood, I will pass over you."

In the Old Testament, God's chosen people sinned grievously against the Lord; but when they repented in sackcloth and ashes we read, "He hath not beheld iniquity in Jacob" (Num. 23:21). We have the sad commentary on Lot, as given in Genesis 18 and 19. Lot stooped to the lowest level—he committed the baser sort of sin . . . the most despicable practice the human race could commit; and yet, after Calvary the Holy Spirit referred to Lot as *righteous Lot:* "And turning the cities of Sodom and

Gomorrha into ashes condemned them with an overthrow . . . and delivered just Lot . . . (for that righteous man dwelling among them, in seeing and hearing, vexed his righteous soul from day to day with their unlawful deeds;) The Lord knoweth how to deliver the godly out of temptations, and to reserve the unjust unto the day of judgment to be punished" (II Peter 2:6–9).

David took his neighbor's wife, had his neighbor murdered in the front line of battle; but when David cried out unto the Lord in repentance and godly sorrow for his sins, as recorded in Psalm 51, God forgave him and the Holy Spirit declares, "Blessed is he whose transgression is forgiven, whose sin is covered" (Psalm 32:1). David is mentioned many times in the New Testament, but not one time is there mention of the sin he committed against his neighbor. David is referred to as the man "after God's own heart."

So we see in the life of Jacob, Lot, David and others that God's love wondrously covers sin when sin is confessed and forsaken. But forgiveness, past, present and future, depends upon Calvary——because at Calvary God was at His best, delivering heaven's best for earth's worst——and only through the shed blood at Calvary can such grace be bestowed upon sinners.

Therefore, if God so loved us, we certainly ought to love Him; and if Jesus served out of a heart of love in order that we might have salvation, if we claim to be followers of the Lord Jesus we should serve out of a heart of love.

The servant is to obey his master "as unto the Lord." The masters referred to here are according to the flesh. Therefore, the servant is to serve "with fear and trembling, in singleness of heart AS UNTO CHRIST, not with eyeservice, as *men-pleasers*, but as the servants of Christ, doing the will of God from the heart; with good will doing service, AS TO THE LORD, AND NOT TO MEN."

I wish I could get this across to all believers who work in public work: According to Dr. Bob Jones, Sr., one of the old-time saints, "IT IS A SIN TO DO LESS THAN YOUR BEST." To every born again person who is in public work, let me say, You may get by with a lot of things. You may play on the job and get away with it. You may say, "Well, all of the other employees take their liberties. They stand and talk, they kill time . . . why should not I?" I will be very happy to answer that for you: The poor unbeliever is working only for a salary ——but my dear brother and sister in Christ, YOU are serving the Lord even though you work in a textile plant, a plastic plant, or any other commercial work. You are on your honor. Your employer may trust you in every detail; and if you kill time on the job you are grieving the Lord. We who are saved are to do whatsoever we do *to the glory of God*. As a believer we should give our employer a good full hour for every hour we are paid for. If he pays us for eight hours and we give him seven and a half, we have stolen a half hour of our pay. It is wrong to do less than your best, regardless of what you are doing. It is a sin for a woman to half-do her housework. A Christian woman should wash her dishes as clean as it is humanly possible to wash them. She should sweep the floor with diligence, as unto the Lord. She should do her laundry as white as snow. It is a good testimony for Christians to do their best.

Christianity is not a fire insurance policy against hell. We are the only Bible this careless world will read. We are God's signboards in a sinful world. Men watch us, and they judge Jesus by the way we live, work, act, and talk. The most menial task——even cleaning out the gutter, janitoring at the church or in a public building

—the most menial routine of drudgery must be done AS UNTO THE LORD, and if we fail, we are not failing our employer—we are failing our Saviour. We are not to do what we do to please men, we are not to do what we do to be seen of men. A person who stands idle on the job until the footsteps of the boss are heard and then runs to take up his tools or his position at his desk, is a poor specimen of Christianity. You should not serve your boss or employer any less faithfully when he is in another city or another state, than you serve him when he is standing beside you where you work! Remember—as sons of God, we are to do all to the glory of God:

"KNOWING THAT WHATSOEVER GOOD THING ANY MAN DOETH, THE SAME SHALL HE RECEIVE OF THE LORD, WHETHER HE BE BOND OR FREE." Think of it! Knowing that whatsoever good we do, if we do it as unto the Lord, we shall receive again from the Lord. The Lord keeps a strict and careful account of all services rendered by His children—from the greatest to the most humble task. The Lord Jesus is a faithful paymaster—nothing misses His eye, nothing is overlooked by Him. The Lord keeps a record of whatever we do—even to the giving of a cup of cold water in His name. Or if, as the widow, we have only two mites to give, that most humble of gifts will not go unrewarded. We will receive "in full" from our Paymaster when we are rewarded for our stewardship.

Jesus Christ is not a penny-pincher, nor is He a miser. In chapter four of the Gospel of John we have a tremendous passage concerning many things as having to do with salvation and our service to mankind in the name of Jesus. Jesus sat by the well as the woman of Samaria came to draw water. He asked her for a drink, and in the due course of time through their conversation, she received living water. While Jesus was leading this woman into the door of salvation, the disciples were gone into the city to buy bread, and when they returned Jesus would not eat. They did not understand this. Jesus said, "I have meat to eat that ye know not of. . . . Say not ye, There are yet four months, and then cometh harvest? Behold, I say unto you, Lift up your eyes, and look on the fields; FOR THEY ARE WHITE ALREADY TO HARVEST. And HE THAT REAPETH RECEIVETH WAGES, AND GATHERETH FRUIT UNTO LIFE ETERNAL: THAT BOTH HE THAT SOWETH AND HE THAT REAPETH MAY REJOICE TOGETHER" (John 4:32, 35, 36). Jesus pays wages for service rendered—and as I pointed out earlier in this series, each one of us will appear before the judgment seat of Christ to receive the reward for things done in our body.

In verse 9, Paul warns the master not to threaten, not to be a slave driver. "Do the same things unto them, forbearing threatening." Paul reminds the masters that they, too, have a Master in heaven, that He keeps a record, and that He is no respecter of persons. He has just as much respect for the slave as He has for the master. He knows no class distinctions. He judges all by the same impartial, divine standards; therefore, the master who is over the servant is not a special one in the eyes of the Master in heaven. They are all in the same category—sinners who need a Saviour; and we are all saved in the singular way—through the finished work of the Lord Jesus Christ.

Before leaving this section of our study, let me point out that you will receive from the hand of Almighty God exactly what is coming to you—no more, and no less. As we sow, so shall we reap. As we treat those who are under us, so shall we be treated when we receive the reward for our stewardship. You may rest assured that faithful service unto the Lord will receive a full reward, while unfaithful service will certainly cause your reward to be burned.

SPIRIT-FILLED BELIEVERS FACE WARFARE

Verses 10–18: "Finally, my brethren, be strong in the Lord, and in the power of His might. Put on the whole armour of God, that ye may be able to stand against the wiles of the devil. For we wrestle not against flesh and blood, but against principalities, against powers, against the rulers of the darkness of this world, against spiritual wickedness in high places. Wherefore take unto you the whole armour of God, that ye may be able to withstand in the evil day, and having done all, to stand. Stand therefore, having your loins girt about with truth, and having on the breastplate of righteousness; and your feet shod with the preparation of the gospel of peace; above all, taking the shield of faith, wherewith ye shall be able to quench all the fiery darts of the wicked. And take the helmet of salvation, and the sword of the Spirit, which is the word of God: Praying always with all prayer and supplication in the Spirit, and watching thereunto with all perseverance and supplication for all saints."

Perhaps someone is asking, "Why would Ephesians, the most wonderful Epistle, the most lofty treatise in the New Testament, descend to a battlefield in the end? Is it not true that Christ won the victory completely and entirely? Are we not in Christ Jesus, and therefore victorious in Him? Are we not already seated in the heavenlies? Is not our citizenship in heaven? Then why should this grand and glorious Epistle that bears us from earth's sorrow into the heavenlies, then descend to the battlefield in its climax?"

That question is clearly answered: There is an enemy

within. There is a traitor in our house. I am speaking of the flesh, warring against the spirit. Let me remind you that regardless of how consecrated and separated you are, you live in the flesh. Never let anyone tell you that the flesh is not still alive. It is true that we have crucified the old man . . . the affections of the flesh and the lusts thereof; but Satan will continue to rear his ugly head until we get that glorified body in the first resurrection.

The first desire of the devil is to damn your soul and see you burn in hell. There is a reason for that, which I have not time and space to discuss here. The devil is jealous of Jesus, he is envious, and he wants to burn every soul in hell that he possibly can. But if that soul comes to Jesus, and by faith in His shed blood is born again, Satan does not give up. He is continually seeking to devour his testimony and his influence as a believer: "Be sober, be vigilant; because your adversary the devil, as a roaring lion, walketh about, seeking whom he may devour: Whom resist steadfast in the faith, knowing that the same afflictions are accomplished in your brethren that are in the world" (I Peter 5:8–9).

Most of us read I Peter 5:8 and then stop. We use the verse to warn sinners that the devil is just one step behind them, ready to gobble them up and damn them at any moment. But dearly beloved, we read verse 9 and learn that we are to resist the devil steadfastly in faith, knowing that the same afflictions "are accomplished in your brethren that are in the world," speaking, of course, of fellow Christians, brethren in the Lord. Job was a perfect man, and Satan accused Jehovah God of paying Job to serve Him. You remember what a terrible, terrible test Job went through——but he came out victorious and climaxed his testing by saying, "Though He slay me, yet will I serve Him."

In the New Testament, Peter loved the Lord and he was sincere when he said, "All others may forsake you ––but I will go with you, to prison or to death!" Yet Peter denied his Lord, cursed and swore he never met Him . . . even though he later went out and wept bitterly. If we resist the devil he will run from us; but if we do not resist him, if we are not alert and on guard, he can certainly devour our victory and our testimony . . . and our usefulness as a believer. Believers are certainly in warfare continuously, and will be until we are safe in the arms of Jesus.

If Satan tried every trick in his ungodly book in an effort to cause Jesus to sin, you need never entertain the idea that he will not attack YOU. He did his best to get Jesus to sell out––but with Jesus there was no shortcut. He finally put the devil to flight by declaring, "Thou shalt worship the Lord, thy God, and Him only shalt thou serve!" Then the devil left Jesus "for a season," but it was not long until he returned and through the religious leaders of the day did everything in his ungodly power to stop Jesus and prevent His going to the cross, bearing our sins in His body on the tree. But in spite of the devil, Jesus marched on to victory.

Verse 10 opens with the word "Finally" . . . that is, "To bring these glorious truths to a close, let me warn and advise my brethren." He continues by saying, "My brethren, be strong in the Lord, and in *the power of His might.*" The only way we can be strong against Satan is in the Lord. All the way through the book of Ephesians we are *"in the Lord."* The only way we can overcome the devil is "in the power of HIS might." You are no match for the devil, I am no match for the devil. We have overcome the devil because "greater is He that is in you than he that is in the world" (I John 4:4). If it were not for the power of the Lord, you and I would succumb to the power of Satan; but thank God, we are MORE THAN CONQUERORS THROUGH HIM THAT LOVED US (Rom. 8:37). But never forget that we are more than conquerors ONLY in Him——and if it were not for the power of His might we would not be conquerors. I thank God that Jesus has never asked me to walk a path that He did not walk before me. He was tempted in all points as I am——yet was without sin. Therefore, "there hath no temptation taken you (or me) but such as is common to every man"; but God is faithful, and He will not permit us to be tempted above that we are able, but will with the very temptation itself make a way to escape, that we poor, weak, finite creatures may be able to bear it——but only *in the Lord* (I Cor. 10:12—13).

In verse 11 Paul begins to instruct us *how* to be strong in the Lord. We are to "put on the whole armour of God." You can clearly see that redemption is the beginning of our salvation. By that, I mean that when we are born again we are a child of God, but we are a *babe* in Christ. We are admonished to grow, and finally, we are to be a good soldier. Babies and children do not enlist in the army. Mature men enlist in the army to fight the enemies of the homeland. Paul takes for granted that the Ephesian believers have grown to the place where they are strong enough, developed enough, and old enough in the Lord to become a good soldier and fight the warfare against Satan. We are to put on the whole armor of God so that we may be able to stand against the wiles of the devil——and his wiles are many, you may rest assured of that.

"The whole armour of God" conveys to us the origin and the nature of the armor. Please mark well the fact that the armor with which we will be able to quench all the fiery darts of the devil is from God——it is not manmade, it is God-furnished. Please notice: The armor of

God is not fancy garments of lace, linen or silk——but *armor*——and when we think of armor we think of steel. Certainly we need the armor of God that we may be able to stand against Satan's methods and escape his pitfalls. The Greek word for "wiles" could have been translated "methods." Satan has many demon-devised methods and schemes to outwit the child of God——and we must have the mind of Christ and the power of the Spirit if we overcome Satan's many "methods."

Before leaving verse 11, let me point out one more fact: We are to put on the *whole* armor if we are to stand. If we leave one spot unprotected by God's armor, if there is one little detail that we think we can handle in the flesh, we are open to defeat. It takes ALL the armor if we are to be able to stand in the hour of battle.

Verse 12 gives us light as to whom we are fighting against: "We wrestle not against flesh and blood, but against principalities, against powers, against the rulers of the darkness of this world, against spiritual wickedness in high places." We are not to deceive ourselves in thinking that our enemy is weak, or that he is flesh and blood. No, we are not wrestling against human power. We are wrestling against demon-power. Carnal weapons of the flesh will not suffice. We may invent weapons galore . . . varied and sundry weapons . . . we may do our best but the weapons we invent will not bring victory.

There is gross ignorance among believers concerning Satan's kingdom. It would do most Christians a world of good to take time out to study the devil and his demon kingdom. The devil is a personality. Liberals and modernists would have us believe that Satan is an evil influence——but the Bible distinctly teaches that he is a person. Jesus referred to him as "the prince of this world" (John 12:31). Paul describes the devil as "the god of this age" (II Cor. 4:4). In our present epistle Paul describes Satan as "the prince of the power of the air" (Eph. 2:2). In the last precious book of the Bible, John refers to our archenemy as "the great dragon . . . that old serpent . . . the devil . . . Satan . . . who deceiveth the whole world" (Rev. 12:9).

The Word of God does not leave us in ignorance concerning the methods of Satan. He achieves his ends through keeping the souls of the unregenerated in the dark. He blinds their minds (II Cor. 4:3–4). He keeps them from "the light of the world" (John 8:12). Paul, writing to the believers at Corinth, warns them that Satan is transformed into an angel of light. He stands behind the sacred desk in local churches on Sunday morning. He impersonates the *"ministers of righteousness."* He preaches a social gospel, denying the blood. He magnifies works instead of grace. He energizes men to parade under the name of Christian ministers, when in reality they are the ministers of the devil. Study carefully II Corinthians 11:13–15. Satan accuses the brethren (Rev. 12:10). He deceives men—even THE WHOLE WORLD (Rev. 12:9). But Satan does not fight the warfare of evil by himself. He has a well-organized, gigantic, powerful empire. In Matthew 12:26, Jesus speaks of the kingdom of Satan: "And if Satan cast out Satan, he is divided against himself; how shall then his kingdom stand?" Jesus recognized the kingdom of Satan. Why then should we not learn all we can about this powerful kingdom of demons, where the devil is chief over all? Satan is the leader of organized "principalities and powers" which are made up of "rulers of the darkness of this world." These powers and rulers are stationed in the heavenlies.

I am sure someone must be asking, "Did you not say earlier in these messages that *we* are seated with Jesus in the heavenlies?" Yes, *we are* seated in the heavenlies in Christ Jesus. I also pointed out earlier in the message that there are three heavens (II Cor. 12:1–3). There is the atmospheric heavens, the starry heavens, and the Heaven of Heavens. The Third Heaven is "our Father's house." Christ is seated at the right hand of God the Father (Acts 7:55, Heb. 1:1–3). Therefore we are seated with Jesus––not in the atmospheric heavens, not in the starry heavens, but in the Father's house . . . Paradise.

Satan at one time was in the Heaven of Heavens with God the Father. He was the "anointed cherub that covereth." Personally, I believe he was the chief of the archangels. I believe that in the beginning, God created Gabriel, Michael, and Lucifer, and I believe Lucifer was the chief. He was the "high sheriff" of the throne of God until iniquity was found in him. Study carefully Ezekiel 28:14–15, also Isaiah 14:13–14. In these passages you will learn where Satan originated.

Satan brainwashed some of the angels, and led them to believe that together with him they could overthrow God and take His throne, and Satan would exalt HIS throne above the stars of God. Of course, the created is always weaker than the creator; therefore, since God created Lucifer, the Shining One, God was more powerful, and He cast Satan out of the Third Heaven. Now he occupies the atmospheric heavens, he is the prince of the power of the air. Eventually he will be placed in the lake of fire (Rev. 12:7–12) and when he is finally consigned to his eternal abode, his activities will be over. He will be tormented day and night forever and ever, along with the billions he led astray and robbed of their right to the Pearly White City because they refused to "come to Jesus, that they might have life." Satan and all of his demon henchmen will be cast into a bottomless pit (Rev. 19:20, Rev. 20:2–3). Satan is a defeated foe . . . he knows it; therefore, he is walking around seeking whom he may devour. He is the archenemy of every person on this earth.

Verse 13 opens with the word "Wherefore." That is . . . "Because the preceding is true, the following is needful."

Notice: "Wherefore, TAKE" . . . not *"make."* There is a world of difference. Man may make armor that looks very strong and capable of defending against the wiles of the devil; but the armor that brings victory is not armor that man can make, but armor that we TAKE by faith, as the Lord God Almighty provides. We take "the whole armor of God," that we may be able to stand "in the evil day, and having done all, to stand."

In verses 14 and 15, the pieces of armor are listed. There is the *girdle of Truth*. Jesus said, "Ye shall know the Truth, and the Truth shall make you free. . . . I am the Way, the Truth, and the Life . . . Sanctify them through Thy Word, Thy Word is Truth." Therefore, the girdle is Jesus.

Next, we have the covering for the breast . . . the *breastplate of righteousness*. This portion of the armor is for the protection of the most vulnerable parts, the vital organs of heart and lungs where a wound would be fatal. For this, nothing short of righteousness will suffice. "Christ is made unto us wisdom, RIGHTEOUSNESS, sanctification and redemption" (I Cor. 1:29–30). "He who knew no sin was made sin for us that we might become the RIGHTEOUSNESS OF GOD in Him" (II Cor. 5:21). So . . . *the breastplate of righteousness* is Jesus.

We have then the covering for the feet . . . our Gospel shoes: ". . . and your feet shod with the preparation of the Gospel of peace." Jesus said, "Peace I leave with you, my peace I give unto you." "Thou wilt keep him in perfect peace whose mind is stayed on (Jesus)." "His name shall be called Wonderful, Counselor, mighty God, everlasting Father, THE PRINCE OF PEACE." Again, we see that our *shoes* are Jesus.

We have a shield——and with our shield we quench (ward off) the fiery darts of Satan. Be sure you do not forget your shield, because it, "ABOVE ALL," is of utmost importance. "Taking the SHIELD OF FAITH . . . ." The shield is faith . . . "So then, faith cometh by hearing, and hearing by the Word of God." "In the beginning was the Word, and the Word was with God and the Word was God . . . and the Word became flesh and dwelt among us, and we beheld His glory as the glory of the only begotten of the Father, full of grace and truth." "Being born again——not of corruptible seed, but incorruptible, by the Word of God." "Verily, verily, I say unto you, He that heareth my Word and believeth on Him that sent me, hath everlasting life and shall not come into condemnation, but is passed from death unto life." Thus, we clearly see that the shield that guarantees the quenching of all the fiery darts of the wicked is none other than the Lord Jesus Christ. He is faith.

Next, we have a helmet: "Take the *helmet of salvation*." What is salvation? "Christ in you, the hope of glory." "Ye are dead, and your life is hid with Christ in God." "Salvation is of the Lord." "Therefore, He is able to save to the uttermost all that come unto God by Him." "I am the way, the truth and the life. No man cometh unto the Father but by me." "There is no other name under heaven given among men whereby we must be saved." The Scriptures clearly teach us that salvation is Jesus——in you by faith.

Last, but by no means least, we need a sword. ". . .

and the *sword of the Spirit*, which is the Word of God."
The sword is the Word. "The Word was in the beginning
with God, the Word was God." Jesus was God in flesh
(II Cor. 5:19). Therefore, the sword is Jesus.

You see, beloved——when we are in Christ Jesus,
fully surrendered, soul, spirit and body, we have on the
armor that all hell cannot penetrate. But if we depend
upon our strength, our ability, our implements of warfare,
we are defeated before we begin. We are no match for
Satan and his wicked kingdom. "Let him that thinketh he
standeth, take heed lest he fall" (I Cor. 10:12). When
you get your eyes off Jesus, and think in your heart that
you are able to overcome the world, the flesh and the
devil, you are in for defeat and a great disappointment.

The warrior is to "pray always, with all prayer and
supplication in the Spirit." We are not only to pray, but
we are to *watch* "with all perseverance and supplication
for all saints." We are to pray for ourselves, and for
all other saints, remembering that we are all fighting the
same warfare against the same powerful "principalities
and powers, and rulers of spiritual wickedness in high
places." When we are praying for others, we are strengthened in the inner man ourselves. Prayer is an imperative
if we would be victorious over the world, the flesh, and
the devil. Today, thousands of young men attend seminaries and schools to be taught how to preach. They
"study for the ministry." Not one time did Jesus ever
have a class in "How to Preach." It is true the disciples walked with Jesus for three and one half years,
and He was the greatest Teacher who ever lived. They
were exposed to the greatest ministry ever to exist upon
the face of this earth; but Jesus did not organize any
seminaries or colleges to train preachers.

Do not misunderstand me. I am in favor of education.

I believe many preachers would be *better* preachers had they gone to school. If I had a request granted to me concerning my life before I was converted, I would wish that I had been saved as a child, and that I had gone to school and learned more about the languages used in the time of Jesus, and the original language of our Bible. I realize that I am limited in learning, from the secular standpoint. But thank God for the few years in which I did attend school after the Lord saved me. God puts no stamp of approval upon ignorance. It is not a Christian virtue to be ignorant, neither is it a Christian virtue to advertise your wisdom. I am afraid education today is doing as much, if not more, to harm preachers than to help them. But what I am trying to say, is this: Jesus did not give the disciples any lessons in preaching, but He did teach them to pray. He said, "After this manner, pray ye," and He gave them the model prayer found in Matthew chapter 6. He further instructed them not to pray as the hypocrites—loud repetition—but to go into the closet and shut the door.

I am for public prayer—but I am afraid not many of our public prayers ever reach heaven. I am afraid we pray them to the people in the room with us instead of to the God who hears in secret. We need to be taught how to pray. I confess my limitation in prayer. I need to know a deeper prayer life—and I think most of us would agree that we need to enter the school of prayer to be taught of the Holy Spirit, who "maketh intercession with groanings that cannot be uttered." Of course, if we do not pray in the Spirit, our prayer is only the saying of words. If we pray in the Spirit, He bears the message to our Intercessor (Jesus) who intercedes in our behalf to the Heavenly Father. Prayer is the greatest weapon against the devil. On many occasions Jesus prayed all night. There is a place for all night prayer—and there is a place where a prayer should be short and to the point. If we pray effectively we must pray according to the Bible blueprint for prayer.

Daniel was a praying man. He prayed to God three times a day. I am sure you know the story of how the enemies of Daniel attempted to get him into real trouble because of his prayer life; but they could not change his habit of prayer. Three times daily he went into his room, faced the open window toward Jerusalem (the city of his fathers), and prayed exactly as he had prayed before his enemies had forbidden him to do so. He did not hide, he did not pray in secret. He prayed as he had always prayed. In the tenth chapter of Daniel, we have an interesting account of how the answer to Daniel's prayer was hindered for twenty-one days by the prince of the kingdom of Persia (Dan. 10:13). The prince of the kingdom of Persia was a powerful demon belonging to the kingdom of demons of which Satan is the head. Two things are taught here: (1) the power of prayer, and (2) it is possible for the devil to hinder prayer. For twenty-one days Daniel prayed, and Satan hindered the answer to his prayers. But Daniel remained faithful in his prayer life--and hell had to move aside and let God's answer through! I know we cannot fully understand the depth of this truth--but nevertheless, *it is true*. I am glad that when even the weakest saint of God goes upon his knees, hell must move back as that child of God enters boldly into the holy of holies by a new and living way . . . the Lord Jesus who died . . . and through His death we have access into the very presence of Almighty God. *But only through Jesus.* He is our Mediator (I Tim. 2:5, I John 2:1-2). There is no man or woman, no church or preacher, or anyone else on this earth who can mediate to God on your behalf . . . only Jesus. Every believer is a king and a priest in the eyes of Almighty God.

217

Listen to these words: "Elias was a man subject to like passions as we are, and he prayed earnestly that it might not rain: and it rained not on the earth by the space of three years and six months. And he prayed again, and the heaven gave rain, and the earth brought forth her fruit" (James 5:17–18). Elijah was a powerful man of prayer––but he served the same God we serve, and if we would pray in the Spirit, led of the Spirit, we too would get an answer from God. One prayer promise: "If ye abide in me, and my words abide in you, ye shall ask what ye will, and it shall be done unto you" (John 15:7). That verse needs no comment . . . it is clear and understood. An abiding believer who is filled with the Word shall ask what he will, and a God who cannot lie nor break His promise nor prove unfaithful, will answer. I know that we will regret when we stand before Jesus to receive our rewards, that we did not talk less, work less, preach less, teach less . . . and pray more! If we would stay ahead of the devil, we should obey I Thessalonians 5:17: "PRAY WITHOUT CEASING."

PREACHERS AND PRAYER – CHURCHES AND PRAYER

Verses 18–24: "Praying always with all prayer and supplication in the Spirit, and watching thereunto with all perseverance and supplication for all saints; And for me, that utterance may be given unto me, that I may open my mouth boldly, to make known the mystery of the Gospel, for which I am an ambassador in bonds: that therein I may speak boldly, as I ought to speak. But that ye also may know my affairs, and how I do, Tychicus, a beloved brother and faithful minister in the Lord, shall make known to you all things: Whom I have sent unto you for the same purpose, that ye might know our affairs, and that he might comfort your hearts. *Peace* be to the brethren, and love with faith, from God the Father and the Lord

Jesus Christ. *Grace* be with all them that love our Lord Jesus Christ in sincerity. Amen."

I have been traveling as an evangelist for many years. I have learned many things that caused my heart to rejoice. I have learned many other things that caused me to be filled with sadness. One of the sad things I have learned is the fact that many churches have pastors who do not preach the Word in power and effectiveness. Members of churches come to me, lamenting the fact that their pastor is weak and lacks power in the pulpit. His messages are anemic, and any high school boy could preach just as good sermons as he preaches on Sunday morning. But very few of these dear people who have brought their grievances to me have said, "Brother Greene, we have prayed earnestly for our pastor, that God would open his eyes and give him power." No church member has any right to criticize his pastor until he has prayed earnestly for him, that God would endue him with power and lead him by the Holy Spirit. I know that personal consecration and surrender is up to the pastor—but we need to pray for our pastors. Writing to the believers at Thessalonica, Paul said, "And we beseech you, brethren, to know them which labour among you (your pastor, your spiritual leaders) and are over you in the Lord, and admonish you; and to esteem them very highly in love for their work's sake. And be at peace among yourselves" (I Thess. 5:12–13).

You believers who belong to a church where you do not receive the spiritual meat and milk that you need and desire, where the pastor only preaches on the surface, never launches out into the deep things of God—you pray for God to stir him, or move him. If you pray earnestly in the Spirit and from the heart, and to the glory of God, He will either bless that pastor and stir him until he will preach as he should—or else remove him and lay

219

him on the shelf or put him in the graveyard! You must remember that Jesus died for the church. The church is the Bride of Christ. He loves the church, and the pastor is the overseer of the church. If he is not doing the kind of job he ought to be doing, you pray for him; and if he refuses to follow the leadership of the Spirit, God will remove him for the sake of the assembly of believers. Oh, yes! God CAN and God DOES move preachers.

In the church at Jerusalem, the first deacons were set aside and ordained, and the Bible reason for deacons is given in Acts 6:3—4: "Wherefore, brethren, look ye out among you seven men of honest report, full of the Holy Ghost and wisdom, whom we may appoint over this business. But we will give ourselves CONTINUALLY TO PRAYER, AND TO THE MINISTRY OF THE WORD."

Some church people are responsible for the "leanness" of their minister, spiritually speaking. They run the pastor half to death, knocking on doors, ringing door bells, and correcting whims and grievances among members. Pastors are called of God to *feed the flock* . . . they are not called to take care of the secondary matters of the church. I know in this day and hour, preachers visit almost continually from morning until night——but I invite anyone to disprove the statement I have made, according to the Scriptures. In the New Testament church, it is the responsibility of the deacons to visit the sick, the needy, the shut-ins, and to take care of the secondary matters of the church in order for the pastor to be continually in an attitude of prayer, studying the Word of God and preparing himself to deliver the message to the believers that will strengthen them in the inner man and cause them to be the kind of witnesses they ought to be. I say this in love and tenderness: Many sermons on Sunday morning are second-hand sermons, copied from some outline book published by the denominational headquarters . . . and that ought not to be! Studying is hard work—but it is profitable in the ministry.

Paul said, "Study to shew thyself approved unto God, a workman that needeth not to be ashamed, rightly dividing the Word of Truth" (II Tim. 2:15). I believe you will agree that Paul was a spiritual giant. Certainly he was well educated. He sat at the feet of Gamaliel, he was a Pharisee of the Pharisees. But he asked the believers in the church at Ephesus to pray for him, that he might be enabled to "make known the mystery of the Gospel." The only way any minister can understand the mystery of the Gospel and the deep things of God, is to spend much time in study and prayer. Every member of the New Testament church should be a prayer partner with his preacher. He should watch and pray . . . "Watch thereunto with all perseverance."

Paul's second request for prayer was that he might be a bold preacher, that he might "speak the truth with boldness." Thank God for that prayer request! You should pray for your preacher, that God would give him holy boldness. We need more "dare saints" in the pulpits . . . men who will dare to follow God if they must risk their physical life in doing it. I know the church today has within its membership demon-possessed hypocrites, church members who have never been saved. They do not want the Gospel, they are not going to put up with it. When their sins are named, they become angry. They set about to get rid of God's preacher—but if God's saints will pray and trust as they should, God can get rid of the hypocrites. He has several ways of doing it.

Paul was in bonds, in chains . . . he was in prison; but he prayed and asked his fellow believers to pray that God would give him holy boldness.

I can truthfully say, "God bears me record; I lie not,"

I have never withheld a statement in the pulpit to keep from offending some worldly-minded church member, some professing person who lives a hypocritical life. After all, God saved me from hell, called me to preach——and even gives me the air I breathe. In Him I live and move and have my being. Every good gift that I have comes from God . . . why should I fear man? I can truthfully say I have never seen a man with a pocketbook or a bank account large enough——nor a fist broad enough——to frighten me in the pulpit. I am not a bully——but *I am* God's preacher. I have had some trying experiences in the years of my ministry. I have been threatened . . . a man once came into my pulpit with a gun. He had been sent by gamblers to shut my mouth. But the next day, God ground that man's arm off in an ice machine! The Bible says, "Touch not mine anointed." I am not a fatalist——but I believe that as long as I live right and preach right, all hell cannot touch me! I pray daily for God to keep me bold . . . that He will never let me compromise, never let me soft-pedal. Oh, God! Never let me sell out!

May I ask every believer who reads these lines, to pray for me? As I speak to you through this printed page, I am forty-eight years old. I have been preaching the Gospel for twenty-eight years. These are troublesome days and perilous times. It is harder to preach the Gospel today than it has ever been. Pray that God will give me holy boldness and keep me true to His precious Word. Pray for your pastor . . . pray for all of God's ministers and missionaries, that God will keep us humble——yet bold and uncompromising in our ministry.

In closing, Paul briefly reminds the Ephesians that he has commissioned Tychicus to carry the letter to them, and that Tychicus will tell them fully concerning the affairs of Paul and his experiences in prison in Rome.

I had the privilege of visiting the dungeon where

222

Paul was alleged to have been imprisoned in Rome, and I stood on the rock slab and I saw the iron rings on the wall, fastened with a huge bar where Paul was chained to the wall in that dark dungeon. The missionary who was with me had a small flashlight, and he flashed the light on the rings through which Paul's hands were locked and handcuffed. As I stood there, the hot tears ran down my cheeks and dripped on the rock beneath my feet. I felt as though I should remove my shoes from my feet, because I felt that I was standing on holy ground. To me, Paul was the greatest of the great. Aside from Jesus Christ, there has never been a greater man than the Apostle Paul!

Paul follows his instruction concerning Tychicus, with a two-fold benediction. To the believers at Ephesus, he said, "Peace be to the brethren, and love with faith, from God the Father and the Lord Jesus Christ." Then reaching out through the church age until the Bride is complete and all born again are caught up to meet the Lord Jesus in the clouds in the air, Paul says tenderly, "Grace be with ALL them that love our Lord Jesus Christ in sincerity." That includes you and me.

This supernal, glorious, greatest of the great Epistles opens with "Grace be to you, and peace from God our Father and the Lord Jesus Christ." It closes with "Peace be to the brethren, grace be with all them that love our Lord Jesus Christ in sincerity." Yes, the Christian life begins in grace, we are kept in grace, and we will stand before God accepted in the Beloved . . . *in Grace.*

In closing, let me plead with every person who has read this book: Ask yourself the solemn question, "Am I saved by Grace?" That is the only way. This is the day of Grace——and if you step inside the Pearly Gates at the end of life's journey, it will be because you received the Lord Jesus Christ by faith——and because you trust Jesus, God saves you for Jesus' sake.

Hear these clear, understandable words: "For by grace are ye saved through faith, and that not of yourselves. It is the gift of God, not of works, lest any man should boast" (Eph. 2:8–9).

"The grace of our Lord Jesus Christ be with you all" until we meet——if not on this earth, then in the City of God. Amen.